THE RETURN OF
JESUS CHRIST

THE END OR THE BEGINNING?

Mark Dunman

New Wine Press

New Wine Press

An imprint of Roperpenberthy Publishing Ltd
19 Egerton Place
Weybridge KT13 0PF
United Kingdom

ISBN 978 1 905991 31 0

Typeset in the UK by **documen**, www.documen.co.uk
Printed in the United Kingdom

CONTENTS

FOREWORD

In the New Testament Paul spoke to many groups of believers about things that were difficult to understand. His purpose was that they would not remain ignorant of the plans that God had for them as individuals who were now part of His Glorious Church. To the Corinthians he said, *"But we speak the wisdom of God in a mystery, the hidden wisdom which God ordained before the ages..."*. There are many matters that begin as complete mysteries to us. But in every epistle that Paul wrote, his aim was to try and explain these things in ways that believers down the ages would be able to understand. Nevertheless, because of the limitations of our minds, we would always be *"... seeing through a glass darkly."* There is the mystery of Christ Himself spoken in *Ephesians 3*; then Christ's relationship with the Church in *Chapter 5* and the mystery of the gospel in *Ephesians 6:19*. *Romans 11:25* talks of the mystery of Israel; in other places Paul speaks of the mystery of sufferings, the mystery of iniquity and the ignorance that so many have regarding the gifts of the Holy Spirit, *1 Corinthians 12:1*, as well as *"Satan's devices"*, *2 Corinthians 2:11*. No matter how long you have been a believer, there is so much more to learn.

What Mark has done in his first book (*Has God really finished with Israel?*) in explaining the mystery of Israel, he has continued in this one as he seeks to explain the Mystery of Christ's Second Coming, but in language that most Christians can understand. *'Behold I show you a mystery'*, says Paul in *1 Corinthians 15:51*, *"We shall not all sleep, but we shall all be changed."* There is a glorious future ahead for all true believers and whilst Satan would want to keep us all in ignorance over what has been revealed to us of the future, we should all be grateful to Mark in his attempt to make that simpler to understand. You may not agree with all his deductions, but if it awakens you like the Bereans of *Acts 17 "to search more carefully if these things are so"*, then it will have done its job.

In our lifetime, there have been many books written on this subject which have often introduced complex and novel ideas to fill in gaps of our understanding. Because of the complexity of theories that have been promoted and the resulting confusion that has caused contention and division, Christians have tended to avoid the subject and just settle for safety in "Pan-Millennialism" which teaches that all things will "pan-out" in the end! But is this really what God wants? I don't think early church Christians felt this way. They were filled with anticipation of the Lord's coming. Read the final verses of each chapter of *1 Thessalonians*, especially *4:17-18, "And thus we shall always be with the Lord. Therefore comfort one another with these words."* So, how can we encourage one another in the terrible times that so many are facing today, without the certain hope of His imminent coming?

This book is a straightforward overview of different ideas and terms used in the debates that have been waged over the years since the Reformation, but especially since the Evangelical Awakening of the late 18th and early 19th centuries. Good use is made of Old and New Testament scripture to support the aim to stir up Christians to *"understand the times"* in order to know what kind of people we ought to be in these critical 'end time' days, *2 Peter 3:11*. If knowledge of the Lord doesn't lead to change of character, then it is not worth knowing.

Ultimately, the words of Amos come to mind: *"Woe to you who desire the day of the Lord! For what good is the day of the Lord to you?"* *Amos 5:18*. This is a challenge to all of us to realise that when the Lord does indeed come back to reign, it will be after the most awful day that the world has ever known. *"It will be darkness and not light,"* says Amos, indicating that the day of Grace is over, and judgment is falling. So knowledge of His plans must lead to responsible sharing with others even in the Church, otherwise we run the danger of being a quirky 'focus group' rather than a Christ-like people who are signposts to the Lord and to the glorious future that He has promised for us.

Rev Derek Rous BA, MBE
Director of Prayer for Israel

PREFACE

The Middle East is becoming a more dangerous place day by day. In the time since I first sent the manuscript of this book to the publisher we have seen the rise of ISIS or the Islamic Caliphate across northern Iraq and parts of Syria. The West has been stunned by the killing of Western hostages and the threat posed by this extreme Islamist group. However, many innocent Christians and Muslims alike have died in the on-going conflict in Syria in the last three years. Israel has once again been involved in conflict with Hamas in *Operation Protective Edge*, as it seeks to stop the continuing rocket attacks against Southern Israel.

The Middle East is indeed a dangerous place and it becomes ever more important to examine its role in the end-times prior to Christ's return to earth. By avoiding this subject there is a danger that Christians will be overtaken by events for which they need to prepare. As we shall see there are very different approaches to the events surrounding Christ's return and they cannot all be right. This book explains and discusses the various approaches and seeks to arrive at the most realistic viewpoint.

There is another reason why Christians should concern themselves with this subject and that is the power of prayer. We cannot expect to change God's sovereign will as expressed in the Bible. What he has ordained for human history will happen, but we can expect to influence events and the way history unfolds. If this were not the case then there would be no point in praying. The Bible is full of exhortations to pray, and on the subject of the end-times Jesus himself said:

Watch therefore and pray always that you may be counted
worthy to escape all these things that will come to pass...
(Luke 21:36 NKJV)

Several times in the Olivet discourse Jesus warns his followers to be watchful, prepared and prayerful.

How many Christians today are in this frame of mind? One view of the end-times holds that since the world is nowhere near ready to receive Christ, his return must be a long way off. Perhaps we need to question this view. Maybe Christ is not going to return to a world that is ready for him. Maybe he will return to a world so darkened and damaged by human sin that it needs radical surgery. If this is the case then his return could be close. That is why I believe we should watch the Middle East and the fortunes of Israel, a theme I shall develop in the book.

The reader may respond: How, or what, should I pray about such issues? I realize that this is a serious question if one is not familiar with praying for world events. Nevertheless one could start with our Lord's Prayer with an emphasis on: *"Thy will be done on earth as it is in heaven"* and apply it to whatever part of the world one feels drawn to by the Holy Spirit.

Part of being prepared for the return of Christ is to know his call on our lives and to be fulfilling his work. Many, many Christians are already responding to the Lord's call on their lives, but perhaps it is time to start viewing this in the context of his expected return.

The words of Jesus make clear that persecution is to be expected in an active Christian life. This is happening increasingly in Christian countries such as Britain where the expression of Christian beliefs and practices is now regularly challenged by humanist political correctness. In more hostile parts of the world this persecution leads to martyrdom for Christians as it has done over the last 2000 years, with increasing intensity in recent times.

We need to pray about this and how we should respond to the possibility of persecution. In short Christians should prayerfully consider their lives and work in the context that Jesus could return soon. If his return is some way off, this issue is not so pressing, but if it is closer than we think then we should be prepared for it. The traditional belief among Christians throughout the ages that Christ could come in their lifetime has been a good one. Pastors have taught them to be prepared.

A word is appropriate about sources I have used for the book. There is a list of reference books in the bibliography, but I have also referenced various websites in the chapter notes. These days the World Wide Web (Internet) is a wonderful source of information and it is increasingly used as a reference source by authors. The web addresses for articles and other materials were all accessible as of March 2015. Sometimes web addresses get withdrawn. When this happens a Google search will usually display alternative websites. Out of print books can often by obtained through online bookshops such as Amazon. However, for new books I encourage readers to support their local Christian bookshop. Information about my first book 'Has God *really* finished with Israel?' can be found on my website: ***markdunman.com***.

Scripture quotations are taken from the English Standard Version (ESV) unless otherwise stated. For dates I have used the more traditional BC and AD (Before Christ and Anno Domini) rather than the modern BCE and CE (Before Common Era and Common Era). There is a glossary which defines theological and other terms used in the book.

I am very grateful to Derek Rous, the director of *Prayer for Israel* for agreeing to take time out of a busy schedule to write the Foreword to this book and for his wise advice. I much appreciate his willingness to do this.

I am grateful to my prayer group *Watchmen for Israel,* for praying for and encouraging me in this endeavour. I am grateful too to my publisher for his professional help and encouragement in this second venture. I should also like to thank my friend Matt for the artwork to my millennial charts.

Once again I am especially grateful to my wife Margaret for her down to earth wisdom encouraging me to stick to a deadline and for typing the manuscript. As with the first book she has several times had to check me and say: "You may understand what you have written, Mark, but since I don't, I am not sure the reader will!" Needless to say this has sent me swiftly back to my writing desk. I hope that, as a result of these interventions, confusion among my readers will be rather less than it might have been!

Finally, I shall leave the reader to decide whether the return of Jesus Christ is the end, the beginning or both!

Mark Dunman
March 2015

CHAPTER ||||||||||||||||||||||||||||||||||||||||||||||||||||||||||||||||||||||||||||||||||||||||||||||||||||||||||||||||

1 *INTRODUCTION*

|||||||||||||||||||||||||| ||||||||||||||||||||||||||||||||||||||||||||||||||||||||||||||||||||||||||||||||||||||||||||||||

The question of the end-times and the return of Jesus Christ at his Second Advent has long preoccupied the Church, exercising its thoughts and hopes. In entering a discussion of this subject I am choosing to go 'where angels fear to tread'. Many distinguished theologians and historical Christian figures have walked this path.

The end-times is a phrase which has come to sum up the close of the Church age which centres on the return of Jesus Christ. The phrase is not found as such in the Bible, but is probably derived from the prophet Daniel's expression *"the time of the end"* (*Daniel 12:4*). It has concerned believers from the beginning of the Church and the writings of the apostles. Various views of the return of Christ have developed centring on the meaning of the 'Millennium', a phrase that describes the 1000 years referred to near the close of the Bible in *Revelation Chapter 20*. There is reason to think that this represents a golden age both for Israel and the Church of resurrected saints, ruled over by Jesus himself.

A golden age that avoids the uncertainty and strife of humanity's condition in the current era of history has led Christians to long for such an age and to hope that it might appear soon. The interest and hope in the return of Christ has been particularly prevalent at times of social and political upheaval during which Christians may have been persecuted. The interest tends to die down during more stable times. Thus, the Church in the early centuries when it was often persecuted, longed for the return of Christ, but when Christianity became the official Church of the Roman Empire after the Emperor Constantine's conversion in AD 312, the hope of Christ's return receded. The Church felt that it had work to do on earth. One millennial view supposed that the Millennium represented the time of the Church on earth and that Christ could not return until the Church had made the world ready to receive him. Another view perceived that Christ was already reigning on earth in a spiritual sense. Nevertheless, as times changed in the face of natural disasters such as the Plague or during times of persecution, millennial 'fever' returned and groups of believers all over Europe came to believe that the end was near, to be followed by a golden age or by eternity.

Why another book?

This subject has been written about many times, so what can I bring to it? As God works out his purposes on earth, the world and the Church change and a new generation of writers arises who bring a fresh view to ancient biblical prophecy. However, that still leaves the fact that most writers on this subject have written in modern times, so I still have to answer the question as to what I can bring!

The first point is that there is always room for a book which summarises and explains the different views on a major topic in Christian theology. Many Christians, both new to the faith and long-standing, are bewildered by terms such as *Millennium, Tribulation, Antichrist, Rapture* and so on. They tend to settle for a truth that is universal to most Christians, namely that Jesus Christ is coming back. It is difficult to miss this in the New Testament, but as to when and how this might happen, most people do not explore, not least because they learn that there is a multiplicity of views on the subject. I would encourage Christians to seek to understand the principal views and then to build on this as their understanding becomes established.

Should we have a view on Christ's return?

Is it important to have a view on the 'when and how' of Christ's return? I think the answer is a definite yes! The subject is not simply one for the theologians. It should concern every Christian, a view that will become clear as we proceed. It matters because the Bible (and Jesus in particular) tells us that we do need to be ready for his return if we are still alive when it happens. Jesus tells us that he may *"come like a thief"* (*Revelation 3:3*) and that some believers will be caught napping.[1] This is especially important if the time of trouble known as the 'Tribulation' is yet a future and not already a past event in history.

As I have studied the various approaches to the end-times I have been amazed at the number of different views that exist among Christians. As we get nearer to the return of the Lord I believe God would want us to have a clear understanding of his Word. Despite the acknowledged symbolism in Revelation and the other apocalyptic books, I do believe it is possible to narrow down the options even if it is unrealistic to expect a unanimous view. It should be possible to clear away the weaker arguments and to indicate that one millennial view is more likely to be correct than another – that is what I hope to do.

A valid approach

What then is the approach which will aid us in coming to a correct view? I think the following points are important:

◊ We need to approach the subject logically. By this I mean we need to weigh the evidence. We should be suspicious of writers, books or articles which talk of 'proofs'. Proof means certainty and in some areas this is not possible.

◊ We need to be prepared to consider all the relevant scriptures, and not just to fit scriptures to our preconceived or preferred plan.

◊ We need to face up to scriptures which may not fit our particular view.

◊ We need to be prepared to say we "don't know" or "are not certain" over subjects where the evidence is not conclusive.

That sums up the approach. There are also what I call *anchor points* for arriving at a correct view of the end-times. Some theologians will dispute these, but my own position is that they are essential to arriving at a correct view:

- Jesus is returning physically to the earth at some point in the future. Very few Christians deny this and rightly so. The New Testament would be unrecognisable if we stripped out the references to Jesus' Second Advent and his own words on this subject.

- We need to understand the Bible as having a literal or straightforward meaning unless it is really impossible to do so.

- We need to treat the Bible as an integrated whole, not giving precedence to the New Testament over the Old Testament and vice versa.

- We need to recognize that God has unfinished business with the Jews as a nation. He has been restoring them to the ancient land of Israel both to fulfil his promises in the Old Testament and to transact this business. (I deal very fully with this subject in my book: *Has God really finished with Israel?*)

Principles of exegesis

Exegesis is the explanation or interpretation of Scripture. In tackling the end-times my over-arching principle is to treat the Old and New Testaments as a coherent, seamless whole from which the following principles proceed:

1. I link the apocalyptic prophets[2] of the Old Testament with the apocalyptic passages or books of the New Testament. For example, I take the writings of Isaiah, Daniel and other Old Testament books, which deal with the end-times and link them with the Olivet discourse of Jesus in the gospels and the book of Revelation.

2. I see a connection between the prophecies concerning the Jews in the Old Testament and the prophecies in both the Olivet discourse and the book of Revelation.

3. I examine the outworking of God's wrath in what the Bible, both Old and New Testaments, calls *the day of the Lord.*

If we play down the role of the Jews or if we do not take seriously the outworking of God's wrath on mankind then I think we end up with both an incomplete and an erroneous view of the end-times as described in the New Testament.

One thing I shall not be doing is to try to predict the outworking of the numerous prophecies except in a general way. This is not a blow-by-blow account of the end-time prophecies, because this is an area where there is genuine uncertainty. I do think we are now approaching the end-times and I will explain why later on. I believe this is so, but I shall not attempt to date any of the events described. The attempts to predict the date of Christ's return have been endless[3] and so far all the historic dates have been wrong!

The Bible – literal or symbolic?

One of the big issues for students of the Bible is whether to take the Bible literally or to interpret it, often with a radically different meaning. My own view is that we should take it literally unless it is clearly written in symbolic language. However, of all the subjects in the Bible, the end-times and the return of Christ are the subjects most strongly written in symbolic language and we do need to recognise this. Nevertheless, because this subject is one that divides opinion among theologians I devote a chapter to the reasons why I think we should understand the Bible literally wherever possible. I do this in Chapter 7 after the reader has had time to assess my approach, but before I come to a critique of the different millennial views in Chapter 8.

Meanwhile it is important to bear in mind that the apocalyptic writings of Old Testament prophets such as Isaiah, Daniel and Joel all dovetail closely with the Olivet discourse of Jesus and the Revelation of the apostle John. It is not possible to treat the respective writings as unrelated events. The theme which holds them together is **the day of the Lord**, as we shall see in Chapter 4.

The book of Revelation

This is the most dramatic and detailed account of the end-times and the return of Christ in the whole Bible. It is important to note that there is an historic view of the book of Revelation as well as a prophetic one. From the Reformation onwards people were able to read the Bible for themselves. During the times of social and political turbulence in the sixteenth and seventeenth centuries in Britain in particular, people interpreted current events in terms of biblical prophecy. They saw the seals, trumpets and bowls of Revelation as applying to their own time in history.[4]

Some theologians take the view that Revelation has both an historic meaning and a future prophetic meaning. This, to my mind, is a much more satisfactory view than thinking that the events of Revelation are now in the past. This approach avoids dispensing with the clear biblical evidence of a climactic close to the present age.

My considered view is that *Revelation Chapters 1-3* represent both individual churches and types of Church that we will find throughout the Church age. I see no reason to treat them as a sequential set of churches in history, since different manifestations of the Church are found in any age. When we come to *Revelation Chapter 4* onwards I think we are still looking into the future. The voice of the one who first spoke to the apostle John said:

> *Come up here, and I will show you what must take place after this.*
>
> (Revelation 4:1)

For reasons that I shall explain I think we are looking into the future, both from John's point of view and from our own at the present time. For reasons that I shall also explain I think we are approaching Christ's return in terms of decades rather than centuries. I am aware that people have thought this on many occasions over the last two thousand years. There are however signs that we are nearing that time.

Biblical evidence

My writing is based on the idea of presenting biblical evidence for the case I argue. This was true of my first book, *Has God really finished with Israel?* and will also be true of this book.

When I wrote about the restoration of the Jews to their ancient land and the re-establishment of the State of Israel I argued that the biblical evidence undeniably establishes the truth of this restoration. To think otherwise demands wholesale re-interpretation of Old Testament Scripture and once we embark on this route, where does it stop?

On the subject of the end-times and the return of Christ I do not argue the case for the view I support with such certainty. I firmly support the premillennial view concerning the return of Christ, but will also present the alternative views. I do not sit on the fence on this subject, but I do recognise that these other views have been around for a long time in Church history. I recognise that within the major positions there are different emphases. For example, premillennialists believe that Christ's return precedes a 1000-year millennial reign, but they have differing views on the timing of the Rapture or the significance of Israel in the last days.

Given the diversity of views on the end-times, it is important to recognise and respect the fact that theologians and other Christians hold their views with integrity. One wise theology professor has said that God has limited our ability to understand scriptural prophecy and that deep humility is needed to approach and unfold it.[5] This becomes especially true when we come to the more detailed aspects of end-time prophecy, such as the timing of the Rapture. The correct approach may be one where we feel the weight of evidence supports a particular view, while recognising that this may not turn out to be the right one.

Conclusion

I want to conclude this introduction by alluding to a very real tension that exists over how Christians perceive the future. This tension exists in the Bible, so it is not surprising that Christians tend to fall into one of two camps: either optimistic or pessimistic about the future.

The Bible has brought us the good news of salvation and Jesus makes it very clear that he wants his disciples to take this good news to the world. In fact we are commanded to fulfil the Great Commission by Jesus himself in *Matthew 28:18-20* and *Acts 1:8*. The optimists take the view that as the gospel spreads and the world becomes a more Christian place, evil will recede.

The pessimists, on the other hand, point out that the Bible itself indicates that there are bleak times ahead with the world becoming spiritually darker. Jesus himself said:

> *We must work the works of him who sent me while it is day; night is coming, when no one can work.*
>
> (John 9:4)

The pessimists argue that evil is not receding, that it is in fact getting worse. How then can we resolve this tension?

The Church has grown at a phenomenal pace in the twentieth century so that it is now estimated that it has around 500 million[6] born-again believers in Jesus Christ. We may be seeing a decline in the Christian faith in the West, especially in Europe, but this is not true of South America, Africa and many parts of Asia. The Holy Spirit is still at work as Jesus promised 2000 years ago. This should be a matter of great rejoicing.

However, we should not presume that this increase in believers means that the world is becoming a better place. There are places where the Christian faith of a community brings dramatic moral and social improvement, but that does not mean that the world and its governments are going in the same direction.

As the reader continues with the book, he or she will find that the principal theological viewpoints about the end-times vary considerably over whether they have an optimistic or a pessimistic outlook. The pessimists may feel that there is little time and little hope for bringing people to Christ or for changing the world before the spiritual darkness descends. The optimists on the other hand may feel we have everything to play for if only we continue to get the message out to the people.

I do believe that only one of the millennial views is correct and I hope to persuade the reader that this is so. Meanwhile I would urge readers not to settle on a view simply on the basis of whether they feel the future is optimistic or pessimistic. If we focus on the spread of the good news of salvation through Jesus Christ I believe we can keep the optimism and pessimism in tension, even though we may decide that the world is becoming a spiritually darker place prior to Christ's return. All viewpoints are agreed that once Christ has returned the world will become an infinitely better place.

I shall return to this subject again at the end of the book when the reader has had an opportunity to assess the various millennial positions.

NOTES

1. See the Parable of the ten virgins in *Matthew Chapter 25*.

2. *Apocalypse* literally means 'unveiling' and was the name given to the apostle John's visions described in the book of Revelation. *Apocalyptic* means pertaining to this revelation; prophesying disaster or doom.

3. A Google search will reveal that the Internet has a ready abundance of articles on date-setting. The following website gives a simple, straightforward account:
   <https://www.raptureready.com/rr-date-setters.html>

4. See Richard Kyle's book, *Awaiting the Millennium* P.71. This is a very good book on the history of millennial views within the Church.

5. Richard Reiter, *Three Views on the Rapture Pre-, Mid-, or Post-Tribulation* P.44. Quoting Robert D. Culver

6. See Note 5 at the end of Chapter 8 where I mention websites which assess the number of Christians.

	AMILLENNIALISM	POSTMILLENNIALISM	PREMILLENNIALISM	
			HISTORIC (Classic)	DISPENSATIONAL
Return of Christ	Physical return to earth. Christ's return leads to resurrection, judgement and the new heaven and earth.	Physical return to earth. Christ's return leads to resurrection, judgement and the new heaven and earth.	Physical return to earth, followed by the Millennium. New heaven and earth after the Millennium.	Physical return to earth, followed by the Millennium. New heaven and earth after the Millennium.
Millennium	Not a fixed period of time – extends for the whole of the Church Age.	1000-year (or an extended) period of time on earth when the Church reigns prior to Christ's return.	1000-year period of time following Christ's return. Followed by final resurrection, judgement and eternity.	1000-year period of time following Christ's return. Followed by final resurrection, judgement and eternity.
Satan's Power	Satan partially bound at the Cross.	Satan's power bound at the Cross and further diminishes as the gospel spreads.	Present age is evil. Satan is not bound until Christ's Second Advent.	Present age is evil. Satan is not bound until Christ's Second Advent.
The Tribulation	The Tribulation extends through history and represents wars, disasters and persecution. It may get worse.	There is no climactic time of Tribulation, prior to the Millennium. (Satan rebels just prior to Christ's return.)	A climactic time of trouble of seven years prior to Christ's return. The Church goes through it.	A climactic time of trouble of seven years prior to Christ's return. The Church does not go through it.
Antichrist	There may be an individual Antichrist.	A spirit of Antichrist, not a person.	A definite person.	A definite person.
PRETERISM	Some Amillennialists.	Some Postmillennialists.	Futurist view of the Tribulation.	Futurist view of the Tribulation.
(Historicist view of the Tribulation)	The events in the Olivet discourse and also in Revelation occurred partially or completely at the time of the destruction of the Temple by the Romans in AD 70.	The events in the Olivet discourse and also in Revelation occurred partially or completely at the time of the destruction of the Temple by the Romans in AD 70.	Both groups recognise that parts of the Olivet discourse referred to the events of AD 70, but not all of it. Most of Jesus' words refer to end-time events.	Futurist view of the Tribulation.
Rapture	Rapture and resurrection of believers happens at Jesus' Second Advent.	Rapture and resurrection of believers happens at Jesus' Second Advent.	Rapture and resurrection of believers happens at Jesus' Second Advent.	Rapture and resurrection of believers is a separate event from Jesus' physical return to earth and happens prior to the Tribulation.
Israel and the Jews	Not significant prior to Christ's return. Israel in Revelation is symbolic. Jews continue to be converted.	Not significant prior to Christ's return (the dominant view). Jews continue to be converted.	Not significant prior to Christ's return. This view is changing now that Israel has been restored as a nation.	Israel and the Jews are very significant in the time preceding Christ's return.
When was this view popular?	Dominant view from 400 AD until the Middle Ages. Still popular today.	Popular from 1600 onwards until the First World War. Popular today as Dominion Postmillennialism	Earliest view of the end-times. Held sway until St. Augustine c. AD 400. Popular again in recent times.	Originated in the early 1800s and has become more popular ever since, especially in the United States.

2 *WHAT IS THE MILLENNIUM?*

In this chapter we will examine the Millennium and the different theologies which have arisen to explain it. We will look at the strengths and weaknesses of the different views in a later chapter. The reason the Millennium is so important is that one's view of the Millennium frames the very different views concerning the Second Advent of the Lord Jesus Christ.

The table opposite attempts to summarize millennial views on different topics. One of the problems in doing this is that there are variations in outlook among the advocates for each position. However, they can be defined by their basic understanding of this period of time known as the Millennium.

Varied approaches to Christ's return

Before I define the Millennium it is necessary to explain that over the centuries theologians have tended to make the circumstances of Christ's return to earth seem rather complex to most ordinary readers of the Bible. This confusion of views has had the undesirable effect of discouraging such readers from trying to understand what the book of Revelation is about. This is not wilful confusion on the part of the theologians. The apocalyptic books like Daniel and Revelation make much use of symbols and metaphors. This inevitably involves interpretation of this symbolism. However, as I explain in Chapter 7, the wise approach to understanding the Bible is to treat its meaning in a literal fashion unless it is really impossible to do this. Even where symbols are used they will refer to actual people and events. I do not believe we should ever mythologize the Word of God. Unfortunately some theologians end up doing this in their approach to the two principal apocalyptic books of Daniel and Revelation.

The book of Revelation

The book of Revelation can be divided into three main sections:

Part 1 Chapters 1-3. These cover the famous letters to the seven churches of Asia Minor. These churches clearly had an historical context, though many writers believe they also represent *types* of church throughout Church history.

Part 2 Chapters 4-18. This is the main prophetic part of Revelation leading up to Christ's return.

Part 3 Chapters 19-22. This is the section describing what happens at and after Christ's return.

It is Parts 2 and 3 which lead to the greatest divergence of views. Part 2 is especially difficult because it is generally agreed that it is difficult to put the events in a clear chronological sequence, though it does end with Christ's return. For example, the first four seal judgements of *Revelation Chapter 6* (the four *Horsemen of the Apocalypse*) seem to be providing a backdrop for the more detailed trumpet and bowl judgements mentioned in later chapters.

Traditionally, there have been three schools of thought about Parts 2 and 3 of Revelation with variations within each school:

1. The Historicist
2. The Futurist
3. The Idealist

The Historicist approach treats Part 2 as having already happened through the 2000 years of Church history. Thus while the return of Christ is still in the future, the events leading up to it have been happening throughout history. The Futurist approach treats Part 2 as still being in the future. The chapters describe prophetic events which have not yet unfolded. The Idealist approach mythologises the events of Part 2 and even of Part 3. The different people, places and events are taken to represent truths which are applicable to Christians in any age. A good summary of these approaches is given by David Pawson in his book *When Jesus returns.*[1]

The Millennial approach

In contrast, I am going to take a different approach to the book of Revelation. I am going to define the different approaches in terms of the Millennium. There are two reasons for this. First, the terms associated with this approach, terms such as postmillennial, premillennial etc., are more easily recognisable than historicist and futurist. Secondly, this approach to the period of time known as the Millennium largely defines whether one adopts an historicist, a futurist or an idealist viewpoint, or even a mixture of any of them. The reader will discern the underlying aspect as I define the millennial approaches. I shall make passing references to Part 1, the section on the churches, but my main emphasis will be on Parts 2 and 3.

There will also be an attempt to dovetail the apocalyptic prophecies of the Old Testament with those of the New Testament and in particular those in Revelation. The objective of the book will be to reach a conclusion as to which is the most realistic approach to the Millennium.

The Millennium

The Millennium is a 1000-year period of time mentioned right at the end of the Bible in the book of Revelation (*Revelation 20:1-10*). It is only mentioned this once as a period of time in the Bible, but several Old Testament passages in the prophetic writings are thought to be describing life on earth during this time (examples include: *Isaiah 11:6-9; 65:20-25*). If one holds to the view that this is an actual time span of 1000 years following the return of Christ, then it is very significant because the Bible suggests that it is a period when Christ himself will rule the earth directly from Jerusalem. This period of time is not the same as the new earth and new heaven, described in the penultimate chapter of the Bible, *Revelation Chapter 21*.

Many Christians believe that Christ returns to earth at his Second Advent to bring the Tribulation to a close by vanquishing his foes and the foes of Israel, and then to proceed to set up his millennial kingdom. However, throughout Church history there has been a divergence of views on the meaning of the Millennium and whether it is a literal 1000-year period. One of the reasons for this is that the 1000-year period is mentioned just one time in the Bible. Some theologians have felt that this puts too much weight on one scripture to support a major tenet of biblical belief. However, the one thousand years is repeated six times in this short passage and there are a number of Old Testament prophecies that appear to be describing this time. For reasons which we shall examine later, these prophecies cannot be describing the later period in eternity known as the new heaven and the new earth. The alternative to accepting that the Millennium is a 1000-year period following the return of Christ, is either to place it before his return or to reinterpret it as meaning something different. This is one of the principal reasons why Christians have diverged in their views concerning the Second Advent of Christ.

Different views of the Millennium

Some writers give a structured and detailed breakdown of the different approaches to the Millennium throughout history. For example, David Pawson does this in the book mentioned earlier in the chapter.[2] While this is an excellent academic exercise, it can also be confusing to the reader new to the subject. For this reason I shall present a simplified overview of the different millennial approaches.

The way that the Millennium has been treated over Church history has led to three major views, each with further variants:

Amillennialism

Postmillennialism

Premillennialism

They all centre their views around the Second Advent of Jesus Christ, but in very different ways. The amillennialists do not believe in a 1000-year span of time, while the post and premillennialists do. The postmillennialists place this period of time before the return of Christ, while the premillennialists place it after his return.

Within the first two there are minor variants, but within Premillennialism there are two major views:

Historic (Classic) Premillennialism

and:

Dispensational Premillennialism

Mention should also be made of **Preterism**. Preterists believe that some or all of the disasters forecast in the Olivet discourse and in Revelation happened around AD 70, the time of the destruction of the Second Temple. In their view of the Millennium they may belong to either the amillennial or the postmillennial school of eschatology.

This may sound very confusing to the person who is new to this subject, but I shall try to navigate a way through, weighing the evidence in favour of the different positions. Fortunately, they all agree that Christ is coming back to the earth. The principal divergence is over when. We will briefly summarise these views and mention some of the historical and contemporary theologians who support each position.

Amillennialism

This is sometimes called **nonmillennialism** because its adherents do not believe in a literal 1000-year period. They believe the Millennium applies to the whole period of Church history between the First and Second Advents of Christ. Since this is now twice the length of a millennial period, the 1000 years cannot be taken literally. They believe that during the Millennium, Christ reigns in the hearts of believers and not through his physical presence on earth following his return. There is not a specific time of tribulation on earth; rather the Tribulation represents the disasters, wars and persecutions that have occurred throughout history. Consequently they take an historical view of the events in Revelation. Many modern amillennialists, theologians like William Hendriksen, see the book of Revelation as consisting of seven sections which run parallel to each other. Each section depicts the Church and the world in different ways in the time between Christ's First and Second Advents. Thus they do not see a future chronological unfolding of events, though they do recognise that the last section (*Chapters 20-22*) takes us into the future with the final triumph of Christ and the new heaven and earth. This eschatological system is therefore known as *Progressive Parallelism*.

They believe Satan's power has been restrained on earth since the crucifixion of Jesus, but think that it will increase as Christ's Second Advent approaches. Amillennialists generally believe that an individual Antichrist will arise, but they do not associate this period of tribulation with Daniel's 70th week (see Chapter 3) or believe that it has anything to do with the Jews. Israel and the restoration of the Jews play no part in their eschatology. Everything in Revelation and the inter-advent period of time is to do with the Church. When Christ returns he will immediately defeat the powers of evil, resurrect the saved and unsaved, judge them and send them to their eternal destinies. This will be followed immediately by the new heaven and new earth of eternity. (*See the Chart opposite.*)

Amillennialists argue that the many numbers in the Bible tend to represent concepts rather than literal statistics: for example, seven represents completeness; twelve the perfection of God's people and one thousand symbolizes a long period of time. Thus there is no need to have the Millennium fit a specific 1000 years.

The amillennial view became the dominant view of the end-times from the time of St Augustine (AD 354-430), one of the most respected and influential of the early Church Fathers. It may have come about as a reaction to the carnal nature of the earth and its association with a literal understanding of the Bible. The Church Fathers in Alexandria, people like Clement (AD 155-220) and his pupil Origen (AD 185-254) came under the influence of Greek philosophy and in particular that of Plato (427-347 BC). Plato interpreted the world at three levels: the body (the literal meaning); the soul (moral and ethical meaning) and the spirit (spiritual meaning). Like Plato they attached most meaning to the spirit and soul and less to the body or literal view of the Bible. Origen in particular was instrumental in introducing the idea that much of the Bible should be understood as symbolic or allegorical.

The amillennial view has remained popular throughout Church history and was supported by the Church reformers: men like Martin Luther and John Calvin. More recently it has been espoused

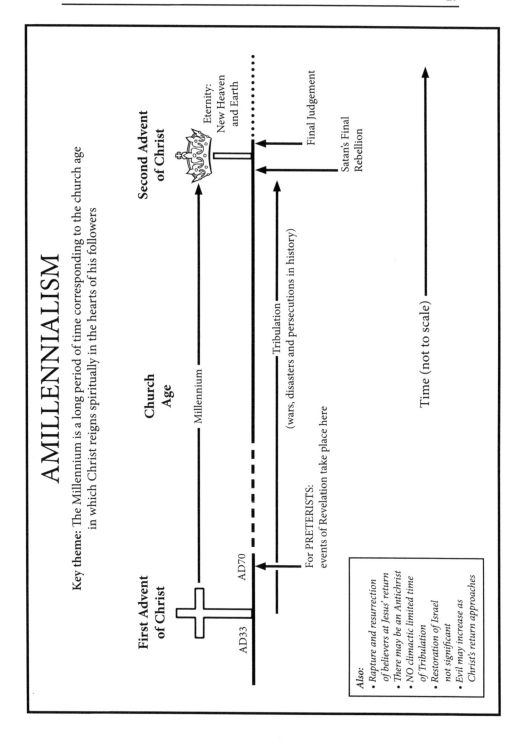

AMILLENNIALISM

Key theme: The Millennium is a long period of time corresponding to the church age in which Christ reigns spiritually in the hearts of his followers

First Advent of Christ

Church Age

Second Advent of Christ

AD33

AD70

Millennium

Eternity: New Heaven and Earth

Final Judgement

Satan's Final Rebellion

Tribulation
(wars, disasters and persecutions in history)

For PRETERISTS: events of Revelation take place here

Time (not to scale)

Also:
- *Rapture and resurrection of believers at Jesus' return*
- *There may be an Antichrist*
- *NO climactic limited time of Tribulation*
- *Restoration of Israel not significant*
- *Evil may increase as Christ's return approaches*

by theologians such as William Hendriksen and Anthony Hoekema. Once people were able to read the Bible for themselves from the sixteenth century onwards, they realised that it was possible to have a view of the end-times other than the official Church view. As a result amillennialism tended to be nudged aside by postmillennialism and later on premillennialism.

Postmillennialism

Most postmillennialists believe in a literal 1000-year reign but think that it will precede the return of Christ. Essentially they believe that with the expansion of the gospel, the kingdom of God will spread in men and women's hearts and find its outworking in the improvement in the way society functions. In short the world will become a better place through becoming more Christian. As more people become Christians this will be reflected in Christian governments as the world is made ready for the return of the King. Christ will return to a world ready to receive him, rather than one which needs his radical surgery.

The postmillennialists do not believe in a specific time of tribulation, nor do they believe in a literal antichrist; Satan's power has slowly waned as people have been won for Christ; it will do so even more as Christian leadership and Christian governments come into place. It is a theology built around the Great Commission given by Christ to his disciples (*Matthew 28:16-20*). This is an excellent approach to our Christian faith, but it does not mean that it leads to a correct theology of the end-times. Where people believe that the 1000 years is a literal period in history, it will be the 1000 years of Christian righteous government prior to Christ's return. Most postmillennialists would agree that despite the spread of the gospel we have not reached this time and the world is nowhere ready to receive the King. It is a millennial view popular with Christians who advocate a victorious eschatology: they understandably see Jesus' call to evangelism as yielding an ever-increasing harvest of souls. Postmillennialists see the Second Advent of Christ rather like the amillennialists. Christ will return, resurrect the saved and unsaved, judge them and send them to their eternal destinies. He will then usher in the new heaven and the new earth. (*See the Chart opposite.*)

POSTMILLENNIALISM

Key theme: The Millennium is a 1,000 year period (or a very long time) prior to Christ's return in which the Church rules on his behalf and prepares the earth for his return

First Advent of Christ

Church Age

Second Advent of Christ

AD33

AD70

For PRETERISTS: events of Revelation take place here

Millennium (1,000 years)

(Satan's power is bound)

Eternity: New Heaven and Earth

Final Judgement

Satan's Final Rebellion

Time (not to scale)

Also:
- *Rapture and resurrection of believers at Jesus' return*
- *NO Antichrist*
- *NO climactic limited time of tribulation*
- *Restoration of Israel may happen at some point in the millennium*

Because postmillennialists see the Millennium as preceding the return of Christ, they are confronted with the statement (*Revelation 20:7-10*) that Satan is released from his prison and will lead a rebellion against the Lord's people. This presents a problem, because the idea of rebellion clashes with the righteous state of affairs set up under worldwide Christian government. The postmillennialists handle this issue in one of two ways. They either accept that there will be a brief rebellion by citizens who have never truly accepted Christ as their saviour, or they argue that it will not be a physical event, but represents a final spiritual conflict for believers. It will be Satan's final attempt to undermine the believers' faith, whereupon he is quickly vanquished.[3]

Postmillennialism became the prevailing eschatology at the end of the seventeenth century. It seems to have crystallised as a millennial view with Thomas Brightman (1562-1607) in his book, *A Revelation of the Revelation*. This view was popularised a century later by Daniel Whitby (1638-1726). It is worth noting that he believed, as did the Puritans, that the 1000-year period would begin after the world had been won for Christ and that the Jews would return to Palestine. The 1000 years would be a time of universal peace and righteousness. Today, however, postmillennialists, like amillennialists, tend to see the Church as having taken the place of Israel.[4] They do not see the regathering of the Jewish people over the last century to their ancient land as being of particular significance. Given what the apostle Paul says in *Romans Chapters 9-11*, they may have a generalised view that God is going to meet with the Jews as a people one day. Like many amillennialists they may be preterists when it comes to considering the meaning of the apocalyptic prophecies in the Olivet discourse and in Revelation. The earliest Protestant reformers had fought hard to retain their independence from the powerful and oppressive Catholic Church. In so far as they believed in an Antichrist they tended to see him in the succession of Catholic popes.

Supporters of postmillennialism include the famous American evangelist of the eighteenth century, Jonathan Edwards. More recent theologians include Benjamin Warfield and Loraine Boettner.

Postmillennialism was popular in the nineteenth century in Great Britain and the United States during a period of optimism. This was the time of the great missionary movements and Christians felt they were evangelising the whole world. However, they did not foresee the parallel growth of evil. For many postmillennialists the First and Second World Wars shattered their optimism.

Kingdom or *Dominion Postmillennialism* has revived the theology of postmillennialism in the last 30 to 40 years. It has grown out of the charismatic and Pentecostal movements and is now a widespread theology in the restoration movement among modern churches. It takes the view that God has been binding Satan through the activities and prayers of the saints. As the Church moves more in the activities of the Holy Spirit, it will succeed in establishing God's kingdom on earth ready for Christ the King. There is no place for an end-time tribulation with an accompanying Antichrist at this time, nor is there a need for a millennial reign of Christ on earth as this will already have happened through the Church.

Preterism is a view that can be held by either amillennialists or postmillennialists. It holds that the apocalyptic prophecies of Jesus (Olivet discourse) and Revelation were partially realised with the destruction of the Temple in AD 70 and the subsequent exiling of the Jews.[5] Some of Jesus' prophecies undoubtedly referred to the Jewish tragedy in AD 70, but not all of them, as we shall see in a later chapter. For preterists the Tribulation is a past, not a future event. The view that the events of Revelation all related to the period around AD 70 conflicts with the accepted theological wisdom that Revelation was written by the apostle John at the end of the first century AD. Revelation from *Chapter 4* was written as applying to future events and this could not have applied to the destruction of the Temple which had already happened.[6]

Premillennialism

In stark contrast to postmillennialism, premillennialism does not see Christ returning to a world that is ready to receive him. Instead it sees him returning to sort out the crisis the world has reached through the rebellion and sin of the human race, and the evil intent of Satan and his kingdom of demonic spirits. Certainly, the world is to be fully evangelised during the epoch of the Church, but parallel to this the activities of Satan reach a crescendo in the Tribulation and the manifestation of the Antichrist. The Tribulation lasts for the specific time of seven years.[7]

Christ vanquishes the devil's agents and locks up Satan himself in the abyss, and then introduces his millennial reign of 1000 years accompanied by the help of resurrected and raptured saints. The earth continues to be populated by mortals who survive the Tribulation. The Millennium thus provides a period in history by which the preceding sinful reign of the human race is contrasted unfavourably with the righteous reign of King Jesus himself.

This period is not the same as the eternal new heaven and earth where Christ hands back authority to God the Father (*1 Corinthians 15:24-28*). The function of the Millennium is to give Christ, who made salvation possible at his First Advent, the opportunity to show humanity how righteous rule should be conducted. Many, but not all premillennnialists, also believe that the Millennium is the time when Israel is restored to its rightful place in God's economy.

Two major strands of premillennialism have developed in history, known respectively as *Historic Premillennialism* and *Dispensational Premillennialism.* A major difference in theology concerns the position of the Rapture in respect to the Tribulation. Another difference concerns the importance attached to the Jews and the restoration of Israel.

Historic Premillennialism

These premillennialists hold the view that the Rapture takes place at the end of the Tribulation, just prior to Christ's physical return to earth. This means that all Christians alive at the beginning of the Tribulation will go through it, many suffering and being martyred during this time while continuing to evangelise the world. They see the Tribulation as the time when the Church will be purified, so that Jesus might receive a Bride that is holy and without blemish (*Ephesians 5:25-27*) at his Second Coming. Traditionally, historic premillennialism has also held the view that Israel and the Jews are not particularly significant at this time; the Tribulation is primarily about the Church and the unbelieving world. They are inclined to be supersessionist in their theology, believing that the Church has taken the place of Israel as God's covenant people, which Jews can join as converts to the Christian faith. *(See the Chart opposite.)*

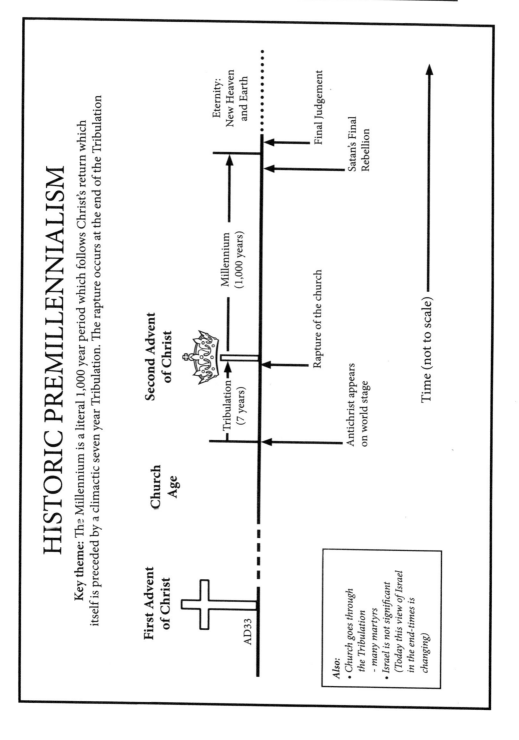

HISTORIC PREMILLENNIALISM

Key theme: The Millennium is a literal 1,000 year period which follows Christ's return which itself is preceded by a climactic seven year Tribulation. The rapture occurs at the end of the Tribulation

First Advent of Christ

AD33

Church Age

Second Advent of Christ

Tribulation (7 years)

Millennium (1,000 years)

Eternity: New Heaven and Earth

Antichrist appears on world stage

Rapture of the church

Final Judgement

Satan's Final Rebellion

Time (not to scale)

Also:
• Church goes through the Tribulation - many martyrs
• Israel is not significant (Today this view of Israel in the end-times is changing)

This eschatology was held by the early Church Fathers in the first three centuries AD. They were distancing themselves from the rabbinic Jews[8] and were thus not sympathetic to the restoration of the Jews as a nation. Premillennial eschatology faded as Church Fathers like Origen began to be influenced by Greek philosophy which tended to see the physical earth as evil and thus to make an earthly Millennium less likely or less desirable. As we saw earlier in the chapter amillennialism became the accepted eschatology of the end-times for many centuries. Premillennialism made a partial comeback in the sixteenth and seventeenth centuries but tended to be overshadowed by the postmillennialism of the Puritans.

However, it should be said today that this distinctive attitude towards Israel and the Jews is no longer watertight. There are now some historic premillennialists[9] who consider that the restoration of the Jews to their ancient land is a significant part of God's purposes for the end-times.

Dispensational Premillennialism

The Puritans, although postmillennialists, were sympathetic to the Jews – it was Oliver Cromwell who allowed them back into England after three centuries of exile. There was a heightened expectation from reading the scriptures that God would restore the Jews to their ancient land. This idea was kept alive by individual Christians over the next two centuries until the nineteenth century when it blossomed into a recent and radically different premillennialism.

Dispensational theology is principally associated with John Nelson Darby, an English curate living in the early nineteenth century, who later founded the Plymouth Brethren. Its hallmark is that it divides biblical history into different ages or dispensations (usually seven) in which God deals with the human race in different ways. They believe we now live in what is called the Church dispensation which will give way to the seventh or final period, the Millennium. They tended to make a sharp distinction between the Church and Israel, believing that at the close of the Church age (the last 2000 years) God would turn his attention once again to Israel. The Church would be raptured **prior to the Tribulation** which would essentially be about God's dealings with Israel and the world. Other than those converted during the Tribulation, the Church would not

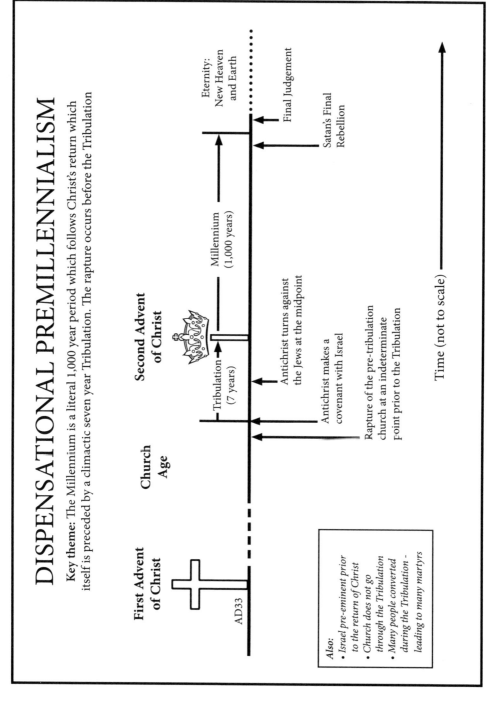

DISPENSATIONAL PREMILLENNIALISM

Key theme: The Millennium is a literal 1,000 year period which follows Christ's return which itself is preceded by a climactic seven year Tribulation. The rapture occurs before the Tribulation

First Advent of Christ

AD33

Church Age

Second Advent of Christ

Tribulation (7 years)

Millennium (1,000 years)

Eternity: New Heaven and Earth

Final Judgement

Satan's Final Rebellion

Antichrist turns against the Jews at the midpoint

Antichrist makes a covenant with Israel

Rapture of the pre-tribulation church at an indeterminate point prior to the Tribulation

Time (not to scale)

Also:
- Israel pre-eminent prior to the return of Christ
- Church does not go through the Tribulation
- Many people converted during the Tribulation - leading to many martyrs

go through it. The early adherents of the dispensational view held to the belief that the Church had failed in God's purposes and he was now looking back to his first covenant people, the Jews – a kind of reverse supersessionism or replacement theology. Christ would return at the end of the seven-year Tribulation and reveal himself to the Jews who would accept him as their Messiah. Having defeated his enemies he would then usher in the 1000-year millennial kingdom. *(See the Chart on the previous page.)*

This then is how we arrive at the category dispensational premillennialism. It is important to emphasise that we do not have to accept its division of biblical dispensations or to accept the now less common view that the Church has failed. Those of us in the Church called to pray for Israel see a partnership in which the Church works hand in hand with God to bring about his purposes for the Jewish people.[10] In this millennial view the Jews are now centre stage to what happens in the end-times. It is also the only eschatology which envisages a pre-tribulation Rapture.

Supporters of historic premillennialism included the early Church Fathers, men such as Irenaeus and Justin Martyr. In the nineteenth century Charles Spurgeon is generally considered to have been an historic premillennialist and several lesser known Bible teachers resisted the new dispensational theology. In modern times the most articulate exponent of this view has been the theologian G.E. Ladd.

Dispensational premillennialists are all relatively modern, starting with J.N. Darby and C.I. Scofield in the nineteenth century, leading on to people such as Herman Hoyt, John Walvoord and Hal Lindsey in modern times.

Conclusion

The subject of the Millennium and the different positions adopted can be confusing. This is not simply because there are several different positions, but because there are variations within each major position. In a later chapter we will examine the pros and cons of each major position.

However, at this stage we can highlight some key questions:

1. Do they take a literal approach to what Scripture says about the end-times?

2. Do they consider the restoration of the Jews to their ancient land as significant during the end-times?

We find that amillennialists and postmillennialists take a more symbolic approach to the Millennium and thus to the end-times, while the premillennialists take a literal approach. This means that the premillennialist envisages a Tribulation of limited duration, a personified Antichrist and the return of Jesus Christ to earth followed by a literal 1000-year reign.

On the second question, the amillennialist and postmillennialist positions do not attach significance to the restoration of the Jews. Their view of the end-times centres on the Church and their non-specific view of the Tribulation[11] means that they do not envisage a climactic end to the Church age in which the Jews and Israel come back into prominence. The premillennial view is the only position that permits the Jews to be centre stage prior to the return of Christ. Traditionally, historic premillennialists have been identified with the amillennialists and postmillennialists as seeing the Church centre stage during the end-times and in not attaching significance to the Jews. However, this premillennial position has shifted in recent years in the light of the actual restoration of Israel as a nation.

The principal view that divides the premillennialists now is the timing of the Rapture. We shall examine this interesting topic in Chapters 5 and 6; suffice it to say here that the Rapture is the meeting with Christ by those Christians who are still alive at the time of his return to earth. They will not die, but will be transformed instead of being resurrected when they meet Jesus. One group believes the Rapture happens just prior to the return of Christ to earth so that the Church goes through the Tribulation, while the other group believes the Rapture precedes the Tribulation and the existing Church[12] does not go through it.

It is important to stress that one does not have to adopt a millennial position in its entirety to arrive at one's own position. The fact that there are variants to all the major viewpoints is testimony to this. The important thing is that one weighs the biblical evidence for each aspect of a millennial viewpoint. I am sympathetic to the dispensational premillennial view because it recognises the significance of Israel, but I am less comfortable with its certainty about a pre-tribulation rapture. While I think its division of biblical history into seven dispensations is an interesting concept, I do not think it has been established conclusively from the biblical evidence.

Later in the book (Chapter 8) we will look more closely at the arguments for and against each position.

NOTES

1. David Pawson, *When Jesus Returns* Chapter 5 – Schools of Interpretation.

2. David Pawson, *When Jesus Returns* Chapters 17 and 18.

3. The contrasting views of two postmillennialists, Kenneth Gentry (actual conflict) and Loraine Boettner (spiritual conflict) can be found on the following websites:

    <http://torreygazette.com/bennuwn/2013/04/08/postmillennialism-and-satans-loosing-kenneth-gentry>

    <http://www.graceonlinelibrary.org/eschatology/postmillennialism/postmillennialism-the-final-apostasy-and-rebellion-by-loraine-boettner/>

    Alternatively a Google search: *Postmillennial view of Satan's final rebellion* will bring up the relevant websites.

4. I explain the meaning of supersessionism or replacement theology in my book, *Has God really finished with Israel?*

5. Preterists fall into two camps: **partial preterism**, the earlier historical view, and **full preterism**.

    Partial preterism holds that prophecies concerning the destruction of Jerusalem, the Antichrist, the Great Tribulation and the Day of the Lord (as Christ coming in judgement), were fulfilled with the destruction of the Temple and the sacking of Jerusalem around AD 70. They distinguish between *the last days* which are in the past and *the last day* which is still future. This entails the Second Advent of Christ, the resurrection of the dead, the final judgement and the creation of the new heaven and new earth.

    Full preterism has consequences rather different to those of partial preterism. It holds that all the prophecies relating to the Second Advent of Christ were fulfilled around AD 70 with the destruction of the Second Temple. This includes the resurrection of the dead and Jesus' second coming. This is one group that does not believe in a future bodily return of the Lord Jesus Christ. It interprets Christ's return as one which was manifested in the destruction of the Temple and Jerusalem, in like manner to the Old Testament descriptions of God coming to destroy nations in righteous judgement. Resurrection of the dead did not entail the raising of a physical body, but instead the resurrection of the soul from Hades, the place of the dead, to exist and operate only in heaven. This view holds that God's covenant with Israel ended in AD 70 and is thus in conflict with any view that believes that God has unfinished business with the Jews as a nation and that he will restore them to their ancient land.

Whereas partial preterism is accepted by some mainstream denominations, no major group has accepted full preterism as a valid theology. (See <http://www.theopedia.com/Preterism> and other websites.)

6.   It is sometimes suggested that the temple John is told to measure in *Revelation 11:1-2* must refer to Herod's Temple, the one that was destroyed in AD 70 and that therefore it was still standing when John wrote Revelation. This is not a convincing argument. The context of *Revelation Chapter 11* suggests a rebuilt Temple at the time of the Tribulation. Jerusalem, the holy city, is said to be trampled on by the Gentiles for forty-two months, a time which would exactly match the second three and one half years of the Tribulation. (For an understanding of the Tribulation, see Chapter 3.)

7.   There have been some Premillennialists who have taken the 'historic' rather than the 'future' view of the Tribulation. They believed Christ would return before the Millennium, but did not believe in a personified antichrist or end-time tribulation. In this respect they were more like the amillennialists or postmillennialists in their eschatology. G E Ladd explains this clearly in *The Blessed Hope* P.32.

8.   See my book *Has God really finished with Israel?* Chapter 10, Replacement Theology.

9.   One such writer is Mike Bickle of the IOHP (International House of Prayer – Kansas City). He attaches importance to Israel, but believes the Church goes through the Tribulation. See <mikebickle.org> (Search for Historic Premillennialism and the Victorious Church, along with Standing with Israel in Great Trouble in the End-times Printed format is available as well as the audio message.)

Readers will find various discussions on this subject on the Internet. Here is just one: <mikevlach.blogspot.co.uk/2011/07/how-does-historic-premillennialism.html>

10. See my book *Has God really finished with Israel?* Chapter 12, The Church's call to pray for Israel.

11. A non-specific tribulation is one that is not restricted to a duration of seven years or even shorter period of time, but one that is spread through the entire church age.

12. This does not include those believers who come to faith during the Tribulation.

3 *WHAT IS THE TRIBULATION AND WHO IS THE ANTICHRIST?*

||||||||||||||||||||||||||| |||||||||||||||||||||||||||||||||||||||||||||||||||||||||||||||||||||||||||||||||||||||||||||||||||||||

Much of this chapter will centre on the book of Revelation and it is important for us to understand the structure of the book. I will expand on the structure of the book which I outlined at the beginning of Chapter 2. *Revelation Chapters 1-3* are about the apostle John's vision of Jesus Christ and his message to the seven Churches of Asia Minor. *Chapters 4-18* are primarily about Israel and the Gentile nations. Although the saints in heaven are referred to several times, the Church on earth is not mentioned once. The Church is not mentioned by name again until the third and final part of *Revelation Chapters 19-22*. This is especially noticeable given its frequent mention in the first three chapters of Revelation.

This is very important because it is argued by some theologians that Israel is not mentioned by name in the longest and central part of Revelation, except for mention of the 144,000 men of Israel (12,000 from twelve tribes) in *Chapter 7* and again in *Chapter 14*. These theologians argue that it is legitimate to see this as a symbolic representation and thus to believe that Revelation is all about the Church.[1] In my view this reversal of narrative is quite wrong. If the Church goes through the Tribulation as some theologians believe, this does not mean that Israel is to be excluded. If on the other hand the Church has been raptured and removed from the earth, then this would be a very good reason why it is not mentioned in the tribulation chapters of Revelation. We will examine the Rapture and the alternative views for its timing in Chapters 5 and 6.

However, I believe it is not sufficient to argue the case that *Chapters 4-18* of Revelation are about Israel and the Gentile unbelieving world, simply through their silence on the Church. Consequently, I present eight further reasons why *Revelation Chapters 4-18* relate primarily to national Israel, rather than the Church.[2]

1. The word *Lamb* is used 26 times in *Revelation Chapters 4-22* and not once in the Church section, *Revelation Chapters 1-3*. It is never used in the Epistles of St. Paul to the churches. It is used only four other times in the New Testament and always in connection with Israel.[3] The death of Jesus is the propitiation for our sins whether Jew or Gentile, but the word *Lamb* has special significance for the Jews because they had sacrificed the Passover Lamb for centuries. It was central to the Mosaic Law. It is no accident of scripture that the word is used so many times in *Revelation 4-22*. God has a message for the Jews in this passage, not the Church to whom he clearly spoke in *Revelation 1-3*.

2. The term *Lion of Judah* and *Root of David (Revelation 5:5)* are Jewish expressions. The first is used only once in scripture and the second twice, all three in Revelation.[4]

3. Daniel is pre-eminently the prophet concerned with both Israel's immediate and distant future. The Angel (thought to be Gabriel) is sent to tell Daniel that he:

    ... came to make you understand what is to happen to your people in the latter days.

    (Daniel 10:14)

    On two separate occasions Daniel is told to seal the book until the end of time *(Daniel 8:26; 12:4)*. The time of the end is described as a time when:

    Many shall run to and fro, and knowledge shall increase.

    (Daniel 12:4)

    It is not difficult to discern that the modern age has vastly expanded both travel and knowledge from Daniel's time in history. It is legitimate therefore to tie these prophecies about his people, the Jews, in with the end-times as described in the New Testament in the Olivet Discourse and the book of Revelation.

4. The prophet Daniel describes a time of great trouble for Israel, known as the 70th week *(Daniel 9:24-27)*. It is associated with *'a king of bold countenance'* who will persecute Daniel's people during this future trouble. It is not difficult to see this figure as the beast of Revelation, commonly known as the Antichrist (see *Daniel 8:23-26; 11:36-45*).

5. Michael, the Archangel charged with the protection of Israel, is mentioned in *Revelation 12* where details are given of his conflict with Satan in heaven. This reflects the clear statement in Daniel:

At that time [the end-times] shall arise Michael, the great prince who has charge of your [Daniel's] people. And there shall be a time of trouble, such as has never been seen since there was a nation till that time.

(Daniel 12:1) [comment added]

6. The woman of *Revelation 12*, clothed with the Sun, with the moon under her feet and on her head a crown of twelve stars, refers to Israel. There is nothing in the text to identify her with the Church. She is not the same as the virgin Bride of Christ described by the apostle Paul in *2 Corinthians 11:2* and *Ephesians 5:22-32*. This bride consisting of both Jews and Gentiles will dwell in the New Jerusalem which comes down from heaven *(Revelation 21:9-14)*. Israel on the other hand is described as a woman and a wife to God *(Isaiah 54:1-6; Jeremiah 3:1-14; Hosea 2:14-23)*. Furthermore, the reference to the sun, moon and twelve stars has echoes of Joseph's dream about his brothers in *Genesis 37:9-11*. This woman is also said to flee into the wilderness where she will be protected by God *(Revelation 12:6)*. This would also match Jesus' instructions to the Jews to flee to the mountains *(Matthew 24:16)*.

7. The time intervals in *Daniel Chapter 7* which refer to activities of the Antichrist and his defeat by God, are repeated in Revelation *(Revelation 12:6, 14; 13:5)*. The time phrases used are: *time, times and half a time; 42 months* and *1260 days*. These are all equal to

three and a half years. We will examine the way the Bible describes time intervals in Appendix 1.

8. It says in Revelation (*Revelation 11:2*) that the nations (Gentiles) will trample the holy city for 42 months. It is reasonable to infer that this means Jerusalem, given that the expression, holy city, is used to describe the New Jerusalem in *Revelation 21:2* and *22:19*, and the old Jerusalem elsewhere in scripture (for example *Nehemiah 11:1; Matthew 27:53*). The seventy weeks of *Daniel 7* are also said to apply to his people and '*your holy city*'. Such a clear reference to Jerusalem in *Revelation 11:2* demonstrates that Jerusalem and thus Israel are right at the centre of the Tribulation described in this book.

These eight reasons together with a failure to mention the Church in the main part of Revelation should establish that this section is about Israel and its relationship with the Gentile nations. It seems illogical to hold to the notion that *Revelation 4-18* is exclusively about the Church and not about Israel. It should be noted that this argument does not establish that the Church has been removed from earth prior to the time of tribulation. I am simply seeking to emphasize that the mid-section of Revelation centres on Israel and its relationship to the Gentile world. It is clear from the text that many Jews and Gentiles will come to faith during this time.

The Tribulation

What then is the Tribulation? We will see in the next chapter that it corresponds to *the day of the Lord,* a fearsome time mentioned several times in the Old Testament. It seems to be a period of history which is still in the future and which will be particularly difficult for the Jews and for Israel as a nation. It will also be difficult for Gentiles who come to faith in Christ during this time and for the existing Church if it is not raptured beforehand. Furthermore, it will be a time of great devastation on the earth in which many people will lose their lives.

It seems that God is permitting this time as a climax to the present era in history with three purposes in mind. First and most important of all, he wants the Jews to recognise that he is their God, to call out to him in their distress and to learn to depend utterly on him. Secondly, and as a means of helping to achieve the first objective, he intends evil to have its fullest flowering. He is even prepared to allow Satan to have 'his moment in the sun' by expressing himself through the Antichrist and the false prophet to demonstrate the utter futility of rebellion against God and its unutterably evil consequences. Thirdly and lastly, God finally gives vent to his wrath both against sinful humanity and against Satan's false kingdom. His mercy for salvation still exists in this situation, but human beings are given a stark choice between putting their faith in God or aligning themselves with the Antichrist (*Revelation 14:9-11*). We shall examine this issue of God's wrath in the next chapter. It is a subject that is often ignored to the detriment of our understanding of God's character and to the realisation that the Tribulation will be a truly terrible time.

I do not propose to attempt a detailed explanation of all the events in Revelation. This has been done many times before, inevitably with a strong element of speculation. Readers who wish to follow a more detailed or chronological approach to Revelation will find books through an online search of the Internet, especially by those writers who subscribe to a dispensational approach to the end-times. (Three such books are mentioned in the bibliography.) What I propose to do is to pick out certain key events and to tie them in where possible with the same events described in corresponding Old Testament prophecies. **It is vitally important to see the connection between the book of Revelation and the Old Testament prophets such as Daniel, Isaiah, Zechariah and Joel.**

The Antichrist

The Antichrist is central to what happens in the end times and so it is a good idea to start by defining him. The word 'antichrist' is used only by the apostle John in his epistles, *1 John* and *2 John* (see *1 John 2:18-23*). The four references in these epistles suggest that the word antichrist is a collective noun – there have been many antichrists. Furthermore, it is suggested that there is a spirit of antichrist (*1 John 4:3*) operating through people, which denies the Father and the Son, Jesus Christ. However, when we examine the book of Daniel, Paul's second epistle to the Thessalonians and Revelation, we find that the writer in each case is very clearly talking about a powerful charismatic individual.

Some people have concluded that John's reference to a spirit operating collectively means that the Antichrist should only be thought of in this way and that there is no individual involved. Antichrist simply means an anti-God system of belief. In my view the biblical evidence contradicts this. Yes, there is a spirit of antichrist, but there will also be an individual. Daniel's **king of bold countenance** (*Daniel 8:23*), Paul's **man of lawlessness** (*2 Thessalonians 2:3*) and Revelation's **beast** (*Revelation 13:1-8*) are all individuals and given what is said about them it is reasonable to conclude that they are all the same individual. This man has come to be called the **Antichrist** for the very good reason that this name exactly describes who he is. He is Satan's response to Jesus Christ, the Son of God.

Satan's history

Satan was excommunicated from his heavenly role as Lucifer, Son of the Morning, because he attempted to be equal to God (see *Isaiah 14:12-14* and *Ezekiel 28:11-19*). Since then he has sought worship. When man, who is made in God's image, was created, Satan sought worship from him. Through deception and lies he caused Adam and Eve to sin, which made them and the whole human race subject to him.[5]

The Antichrist and his false prophet are the very acme of this satanic counterfeit kingdom. People who accept the mark of the beast (*Revelation 13:16-18*) really will be worshipping Satan through his false Christ.

The Antichrist and the seven-year Tribulation

As we saw earlier in the chapter the Tribulation is a time of great trouble for the Jews and the nation of Israel. It is centred on Jerusalem, the holy city, but as the Antichrist consolidates his power, his malevolent influence spreads to cover the whole earth.

> And authority was given it [the beast] over every tribe and people and language and nation...
>
> (Revelation 13:7) [comment added]

It is important to recognise that the Antichrist acquires power over time. It does not happen in a moment. It is also clear, as we shall see, that there is plenty of resistance to his rise to the top.

The period of time from the rise of the Antichrist to his demise at the hands of the Lord Jesus Christ himself has been identified as seven years. We shall examine the biblical approach to intervals of time in Appendix 1, but suffice it to say for the moment that the seventy weeks of Daniel (*Chapter 9*) are considered to be seventy units of seven years. The seventieth week is clearly defined as the time of trouble and this equals seven years.

This week of seven years is further divided into two equal halves and the second half is sometimes known as **The Great Tribulation**, after Jesus' words in *Matthew 24:21*. Let us see how we arrive at this conclusion by returning to the book of Daniel. Of the prince referred to in *Daniel 9:26* it is said:

> And he shall make a strong covenant with many for one week, and for half of the week he shall put an end to sacrifice and offering. And on the wing of abominations shall come one who makes desolate, until the decreed end is poured out on the desolator.
>
> (Daniel 9:27)

Before we unpack this verse, let us first examine why it does not refer to the destruction of the Temple under the Roman General Titus in AD 70. The Romans did not make an agreement (covenant) with the besieged Jews in Jerusalem. They laid siege to the city until they could enter it. They did not close down sacrifice and offering while keeping the Temple in operation. They simply destroyed the Temple. Finally, no decreed end was poured out on the desolator. The Jews were horribly defeated and went into exile, while the Roman Empire continued to flourish for several centuries.[6]

The first part of the verse suggests that the Antichrist makes a covenant with the Jews (involving other nations) for a period of seven years, which allows him into the nation of Israel and into Jerusalem in particular. The implication of the next part of the verse is that the Temple with its sacrifices and offerings has been rebuilt and put into practice, perhaps under the aegis of this Prince. This is not a surprising conclusion because it is what many orthodox Jews wish to see. For almost 2000 years they have been unable to practice their traditional Judaism. The fact that they are once again practising traditional Temple worship is revealed in other biblical passages, as we shall see shortly.[7]

The next part of the above verse indicates that this same prince puts an end to the Temple worship for three and a half years. This suggests that this worship has been permitted from the rebuilding of the Temple until the midpoint of the seven-year Tribulation and then abruptly stopped. These conclusions are supported by the Olivet discourse. Jesus says:

> So when you see the abomination of desolation spoken of by the prophet Daniel, standing in the holy place... then let those who are in Judea flee to the mountains.
>
> (Matthew 24:15-16)

Later he says:

> For then there will be great tribulation, such as has not been from the beginning of the world until now, no, and never will be.
>
> (Matthew 24:21)

This statement ties *verse 15* into this terrible time of tribulation. Bad as it was, there is no way that the destruction of the Temple in AD 70 can be described in these terms.[8] **This verse alone should establish that the Tribulation is a climactic time of trouble, of limited duration, at the close of this age**.

Furthermore, there are several passages in Revelation which describe this time in graphic detail. *Revelation 13* describes the power given to the beast and his false prophet, and how the latter causes people to create an image of the beast to be worshipped. The beast is allowed to exercise authority for 42 months (in other words three and a half years), the same time period that we have just seen in Daniel when the Temple sacrifice and offering is made to cease. Daniel says about this king (prince):

> And the king shall do as he wills. He shall exalt himself and magnify himself above every god, and shall speak astonishing things against the God of gods... he shall magnify himself above all.
>
> (Daniel 11:36-37)

What better place to do this than the Jewish Temple?

One Premillennial view of the Tribulation

The view of many premillennialists for this time of Tribulation can be summed up as follows, with what I recognise are some speculative comments.

Israel reaches a crisis point in its relationship with its Arab neighbours. It is threatened on all sides. Into this situation comes a man who seems able to resolve the Middle East crisis and to enter into a covenant with Israel and its neighbours. To achieve this alone he would be considered something of a miracle worker. However, the realisation of this agreement may in practice be more mundane. Daniel indicates that the king will not have it all his own way (Daniel 11:40-45). He will have to fight ruthlessly to defeat both the king of the south and the king of the north. Then he will be free to enter Israel:

> He shall come into the glorious land.
>
> (Daniel 11:41)

He establishes his dominance over the nations by acting on behalf of the Jews. In the first three and a half years he appears to be on their side:

> *And he shall pitch his palatial tents between the sea and the*
> *glorious holy mountain [Jerusalem].*
>
> *(Daniel 11:45)* [comment added]

Up to this point this king (the beast or Antichrist) does not have the dominance that he has in the second interval of three and a half years, so graphically described in *Revelation 13*. He starts as an ordinary human being.

I will not speculate on the Antichrist's origins.[9] The important thing is that he comes to Israel and Jerusalem. Scripture does not indicate that he fights the Jews to start with. The scriptures just quoted in Daniel suggest the opposite, that he comes as a friend of Israel and temporarily resolves the Middle East crisis, but does not do so without opposition from the surrounding nations.

The rebuilding of the Temple

The idea that the Temple is rebuilt in this period comes not from direct observation of Scripture, but by deduction. Several passages indicate that the Temple will be desecrated, in much the same way as it was by Antiochus Epiphanes in 167 BC. For this to happen there must be a Temple in place and since one no longer exists it will need to be rebuilt. The only realistic time for this rebuilding is the first three and a half years of the Tribulation when the Antichrist is still on the side of the Jews. There is no way that this could happen at the present time. The Muslim authorities lay claim to the Temple Mount in Jerusalem, and any attempt to challenge this would lead to war between Israel and the Arab nations.[10]

The great change in attitude to himself and towards the Jews comes halfway through the Tribulation period. *Revelation 13* refers to a mortal wound from which the beast makes a miraculous recovery:

> *... but its mortal wound was healed, and the whole earth*
> *marvelled as they followed the beast.*
>
> *(Revelation 13:3)*

Some Christian writers have speculated that this is the turning point in the beast's attitude, but we cannot know for certain. What we do know is that the Antichrist now starts to behave like God, as we saw earlier. This is made clear in *Daniel 11:36-39* and *Revelation 13*. He will be a man of violence. Many of those who refuse to worship him or receive the mark of the beast will be killed (*Revelation 13:16-18*).[11] He is allowed to exercise this power for 42 months (*Revelation 13:5*).

Flight of the Jews

The Antichrist now turns his sights on the Jews, but God has prepared a place of hiding in the wilderness for some at least of Israel's people, possibly in the ancient areas of Edom and Moab. They are instructed by Jesus to flee to the mountains once they see the abomination of desolation in the Temple (*Matthew 24:16-20*). This is followed by the Great Tribulation – the second half of the seven-year period:

> *For then there will be **great tribulation**, such as has not been from the beginning of the world until now, no, and never will be. And if those days had not been cut short, no human being would be saved. But for the sake of the elect those days will be cut short.*
>
> (*Matthew 24:21-22*) [emphasis added]

The detail is filled out in *Revelation 12* where we are told that following the war in heaven Satan and his angels are cast down to earth. Satan, in great wrath (*Revelation 12:12*) sets out to pursue the woman, but it says:

> *But the woman was given the two wings of the great eagle so that she might fly from the serpent into the wilderness, to the place where she is to be nourished for a time, and times, and half a time [namely three and a half years].*
>
> (*Revelation 12:14*) [comment added]

We have already seen at the beginning of the chapter (Item 6) that this woman is likely to represent Israel. In the symbolic language that follows the above verse, it seems that the serpent (Satan) pursues the woman, but fails in this endeavour and gives up the pursuit. Instead he goes off to make war on her offspring, described as:

> ... *those who keep the commandments of God and hold to the testimony of Jesus.*
>
> *(Revelation 12:17)*

The population of Jews who flee into the wilderness are protected by God from the predations of Satan, for the whole of this three and a half year period. How this is achieved and why the Antichrist (Satan's chief representative on earth at this time) ceases to pursue them is not explained. I acknowledge that the people with whom Satan goes off to make war are going to be Christians, because they hold to the testimony of Jesus. This could be the Church still on the earth, or it could be believers who have come to faith since the start of the Tribulation and are located across the world. The woman, however, who is located nearby in the Middle East, must represent Israel and the Jewish people.

Evangelism by the Jews

Prior to this midpoint in the Tribulation and the desecration of the Temple, God, through an angel, is described as having sealed 144,000 Jewish men (12,000 from each tribe except Dan) in *Revelation Chapter 7*. The fact that the four angels are told to delay the wrath of God until these people have been sealed, suggests that they survive the Tribulation. This is further confirmed in *Revelation 14* where they are seen with the Lamb (Jesus) on Mount Zion. These are described as having been redeemed from earth and there is no mention of their martyrdom.

They are described in *Revelation 7* as being servants of God. It has been surmised that these 144,000 Jewish men are commissioned to evangelise the world during the terrible times of the Tribulation, a realisation perhaps of Paul's words in Romans:

> *For if their [the Jews] rejection means the reconciliation of the world, what will their acceptance mean but life from the dead?*
> *(Romans 11:15)* [comment added]

Perhaps, and this is supposition, we shall find a reversal of roles. It will be the Jews who evangelise the Gentiles, rather than the Gentiles evangelising the Jews during this time.

God's wrath

Alongside the activities involving the Antichrist and Israel, we also find many passages, especially in Revelation, which describe the pouring out of God's wrath on sinful humanity. This is a subject that is neglected by many millennial writers. If one believes, for example, that the events of Revelation were completed with the destruction of Jerusalem in AD 70, or that the whole of Church history has experienced this outworking of God's wrath, then one misses the acute intensity of the seven-year Tribulation as described in Revelation or the Old Testament passages referring to the **'day of the Lord'**. The earth will be a very unpleasant place in which to dwell during this time. The destruction and loss of life will be immense and individuals will be fortunate to live through it. We will examine the issue of God's wrath in the next chapter. For those who still doubt that there will be a short, climactic time of tribulation at the end of the age, I would draw their attention to Jesus' words quoted earlier in the chapter: *Matthew 24:21-22*. Bad as the destruction of the Temple and Jerusalem were in AD 70 and AD 135, this cannot be compared to the enormity of the time described by Jesus in these verses.

NOTES

1. This is the view of William Hendriksen in *More than Conquerors*, his amillennial exposition of the book of Revelation. On Page 111 he says: "It is very clear, therefore, that the sealed multitude [of 144,000 men of Israel] of Revelation 7 symbolises the entire Church militant of the old and new dispensations." [comment added]

2. I have drawn on F J Dake's Annotated Reference Bible for some of these arguments, referring to his comments on *Revelation*.

3. The four references are: *John 1:29* and *36*; *Acts 8:32* (a quote from *Isaiah 53:7*) and *1 Peter 1:19.*

4. One of these references is *Revelation 22:16* – and here the churches are mentioned.

5. It is an interesting fact that when Satan tempted Jesus for the third time with an offer of the world's human kingdoms, they were his to give. Jesus did not deny this, but simply reminded the devil that God was the only one to be worshipped (*Matthew 4:8-10*).

6. There were two major Jewish revolts against the Romans around the end of the first century AD. The first revolt in AD 66 led to the Jewish War in which the Jews were finally defeated in AD 70. Thousands of Jews died in the war and the siege of Jerusalem. The Temple was destroyed along with much of the city. Of those who survived many were taken captive to Rome. (The Jewish historian, Flavius Josephus, puts the figure at about 90,000.) The second revolt was in AD 132, led by Simon Bar Kochba and finally crushed in AD 135. This time Jerusalem was ransacked. It was renamed Aelia Capitolina and rebuilt as a Roman city. Israel was renamed Syria Palaestina to remove all trace of its Jewishness!

7. At the present time the idea of a Jewish temple on the Temple Mount is quite out of the question. However, it is worth noting that a new Temple could be built on the north side of the Temple Mount, without the need to destroy the Dome of the Rock and the Al-Aqsa Mosques. It is pure speculation, but this could be the sort of solution the Antichrist might broker with Israel's neighbours, especially from a position of strength.

8. It is true that believers fled to the hideout in Pella in AD 70 and in doing so they were probably responding to Jesus' words, but the context of this instruction to flee clearly refers to what happens in the future Tribulation. We shall see shortly that the Jews who flee at this time will be protected for three and a half years in the wilderness.

9. Many people think the Antichrist arises in Europe, from a revival of the old Roman Empire. Others think that he is a successor to the Seleucid kings of Syria. Syria became a province of the old Roman Empire.

10. Most people are not aware that the Israeli authorities have to exercise great vigilance in foiling occasional attempts to blow up the Temple Mount mosques by extremist orthodox Jews.

11. In today's world it is quite feasible that this identity mark might be a microchip inserted under the skin.

4 *THE DAY OF THE LORD AND GOD'S WRATH*

||||||||||||||||||||||||| |||||||||||||||||||||||||||||||||||||||||||||||||||||||||||||||||||||||||||||||||||||||||||||||

It is critical for a correct understanding of the end-times and the return of the Lord Jesus Christ to understand that history is reaching a crescendo with an outpouring of God's wrath on sinful humanity. The scriptures make clear that this is way beyond the localised expression of God's wrath. We see many examples of this localised anger in the Old Testament in relation to sin; for example, God's judgement of Sodom and Gomorrah (*Genesis Chapter 19*) and his fury at the incident of the Golden Calf in Exodus (*Exodus Chapter 32*). However, we also see that God tempered his anger in response to intercession. We know that he would have withheld judgement on Sodom if he had found just ten righteous people (*Genesis 18:22-33*). We know too that following Moses' intercession, he relented over his decision to destroy the Israelites for their golden calf idolatry (*Exodus 32:11-14*).

Time and again in the Old Testament God calls upon Israel's people to repent, so that he does not have to punish them by exile. He hopes even up to the last moment, that Judah will turn back to him (*Jeremiah 26:3; 36:3*). God describes himself as merciful and slow to anger (*Exodus 34:6*).

God's universal wrath in history

However, twice in history God's mercy is exhausted and his wrath boils over.[1] The first occasion was the Noahic Flood (*Genesis Chapters 6-8*) where God regretted that he had made the human race because of the evil in man's heart. This grieved him greatly and only Noah and his family were deemed worthy of being spared the flood. God's mercy came to an end for the rest of humanity and they were all destroyed.

The second occasion is yet in the future and corresponds to the Tribulation. It is also spoken of as **the day of the Lord**, an interval of time which culminates in the day when the Lord Jesus returns to earth. This interval represents a climax or crescendo to what has gone before. The day of the Lord may be an interval of time, but it is not a period of history. Nothing in the description suggests a drawn out period of time, but rather a climax in history. (Likewise, the texts indicate an interval of time rather than a single day.)

With Christ's death and resurrection God opened the way for humanity to be reconciled to him. Jesus took the punishment for our sins, so that we could be clothed in his righteousness and stand in the presence of a holy God. God has used the last 2000 years, the Church age, to call men and women to repentance. He has shown forbearance in his judgement of sin. The apostle Peter says:

> The Lord... is patient towards you, not willing that any should perish, but that all should reach repentance.
>
> (2 Peter 3:9)

Likewise the apostle Paul says:

> The times of ignorance God overlooked, but now he commands all people everywhere to repent, because he has fixed a day on which he will judge the world in righteousness by a man whom he has appointed...
>
> (Acts 17:30-31)

These verses speak of a time of grace, while God waits for people to respond, but they also indicate that his patience is not limitless. It is perhaps worth reminding ourselves that there is another side to God's character which runs alongside his great mercy and love. This is revealed clearly by the prophet Nahum in these sobering words:

> The Lord is a jealous and avenging God; the Lord is avenging and wrathful; the Lord takes vengeance on his adversaries and

keeps wrath for his enemies. The Lord is slow to anger and
great in power, and the Lord will by no means clear the guilty.

(Nahum 1:2-3)

If we believe that the Tribulation has been unfolding over the last
2000 years, or that it is already past, completed perhaps at the time of the
destruction of the Temple in AD 70, then we miss the clear indication of
scripture that God's wrath reaches a climax in *"the great and awesome*
day of the Lord" (Joel 2:31; Malachi 4:5). The word awesome is translated
'terrible' or 'dreadful' in some versions of the Bible.

The sense of certain Old Testament prophecies, the Olivet discourse
of Jesus and above all the book of Revelation, is one of a climax of
wrath unleashed upon the world. This is not to deny that human
history since the time of Christ has been a history of terrible events:
persecution of Jews, persecution of believing Christians (often by the
nominal Christian Church), wars, famines and plagues which all add
up to a grim catalogue of human suffering. The decimation of the
population by the Justinian Plague in the sixth century AD and by the
Black Death in the fourteenth century AD[2] certainly echo the death
toll of the tribulation described in Revelation. However, this tribulation
speaks of a concentrated time when God's wrath is poured out on
sinful humanity. It is the climax of evil in history and God's judgement
of sin. The Antichrist is Satan's attempt to imitate God's Son, but God
permits this travesty in order to contrast the climax of man's evil in the
world with the righteousness of the true Christ, this time appearing as
a triumphant King, and not as the Suffering Servant as he did at his
First Advent.

If the suffering of history has been as great as it has to date, this
should cause us to take a very sober view of God's wrath and judgement
as it reaches a climax at the end of the age.

The day of the Lord

Let us now look at the Bible's description of *the day of the Lord.*
This event and its associated wrath are mentioned both in the Old
and New Testaments. The link between what is described in the Old

Testament passages with the events in the Olivet discourse and the book of Revelation, is impossible to miss.

We first meet *the day of the Lord* in *Isaiah 2:12-22.* Two things are interesting about this reference. The first is that it is described as a day that is *"against all that is proud and lofty, against all that is lifted up – and it shall be brought low."* God hates the pride of man. The second interesting thing is that *verses 19* and *21* are remarkably similar to *Revelation 6:15-16.* People are described as hiding themselves in caves to avoid the terror of the Lord or, in Revelation, the wrath of the Lamb (the Lord Jesus).

In *Isaiah 13:6-13* we have another reference to *the day of the Lord* and its associated destruction. Once again *verses 10-13* bear a remarkable similarity to *Revelation 8:12* where the sun, moon and stars are described as being darkened. *Isaiah 13:12* is a chilling verse: *"I will make people more rare than fine gold."* This echoes the great loss of life described at various points in Revelation.

Yet again when we come to Joel, he speaks of *"the great and awesome day of the Lord"* (*Joel 2:30-31*) which is associated with wonders in heaven and on earth that include the sun being turned to darkness and the moon to (the colour of) blood. This great day is linked to Jerusalem, for it says: *"For in Mount Zion and Jerusalem there shall be those who escape as the Lord has said, and among the survivors shall be those whom the Lord calls."* (verse 32).

Amos 5:18 describes *the day of the Lord* as a day of *"darkness, and not light"*, while *Zephaniah 1:14-18* gives a most graphic description of the wrath of God on the whole of mankind for its sin, once again referring to its darkness and gloom. The Old Testament completes its reference to *the day of the Lord* in *Malachi 4:5* calling it, as Joel does *"the great and awesome day of the Lord."*

Jacob's trouble

There is also another reference to *the day of the Lord* under the name of *Jacob's trouble* in a passage from Jeremiah in which the Lord spoke concerning Israel and Judah:

> *Alas! For that day is great, so that none is like it: it is even the time of **Jacob's trouble**; but he shall be saved out of it.*
>
> (Jeremiah 30:7 KJV) [emphasis added]

This is especially interesting because it clearly ties Israel into the time of tribulation saying that despite the trouble (*distress* in other versions), Israel will be saved out of it. A time of trouble is referred to by the prophet Daniel (*Daniel 12:1*) such as has never been seen before, but again Israel (Daniel's people) will be delivered from it.

God's wrath in the New Testament

This same theme of God's wrath and judgement continues in the New Testament. Thus Paul writes in Thessalonians:

> ... *the day of the Lord will come like a thief in the night. While people are saying, "there is peace and security", then sudden destruction will come upon them as labour pains come upon a pregnant woman, and they will not escape.*
>
> (*1 Thessalonians 5:2-3*)

While Jesus does not refer specifically to *the day of the Lord* in his Olivet discourse (*Matthew 24:3-22*), he ties his return to this day and to the apocalyptic events of Revelation. The disciples say:

> *Tell us, when will these things be, and what will be the sign of your coming and of the close of the age?*
>
> (*Matthew 24:3*)

Towards the end of his response, Jesus says:

> *For then there will be great tribulation, such as has not been from the beginning of the world until now, no, and never will be. And if those days had not been cut short, no human being would be saved. But for the sake of the elect those days will be cut short.*
>
> (*verses 21-22*)

Later he says:

Immediately after the tribulation of those days the sun will be darkened, and the moon will not give its light, and the stars will fall from heaven, and the powers of the heavens will be shaken.

(verse 29)

He then says that this will be followed by the return of the Son of Man in power and great glory.

Jesus' discourse fits the description of *the day of the Lord* in the Old Testament and once again ties the events it describes into the book of Revelation. We see the effects of this time on the light of the sun and the moon – a consistent theme as we study *the day of the Lord*. Some writers have speculated that this darkening of the sun, moon and stars may be the result of nuclear war with all the debris it throws up into the atmosphere, leading to what is popularly known as 'nuclear winter' on the earth – but this is supposition.

We also see the climax to the Tribulation identified with *Revelation Chapter 19* where Jesus returns in power and glory, defeats the enemies arrayed against him and disposes of the Antichrist and false prophet (*Revelation 19:11-21*). This event is the climax to *the day of the Lord*.

Jesus' reference to the need to cut short the days, if life is to be preserved, reflects what we have read in the Old Testament passage from Isaiah (*Isaiah 13:6-13*).

Convincing parallels between the Old and New Testaments

These parallels in the Old and New Testament are so striking that it seems to me to fly in the face of the evidence not to recognise their reference to the same events at the close of the age prior to the return of the Lord Jesus Christ. I think we can reasonably conclude that the Tribulation is a climactic time of God's wrath.[3] The wrath is dispensed on earth at a time when people have consciously and actively rejected God, where disregard for God's laws is rampant and where evil has been allowed to grow and reach its epitome in Satan's manifestation through his false Christ (the Antichrist) and his false prophet. Human beings suffer both through the activities of Satan's representatives on earth and through God's direct wrath ministered by his angels through the Seal, Trumpet and Bowl Judgements described in Revelation. It is not a good time to be on earth!

The enactment of God's wrath

As I said at the end of the previous chapter the subject of God's wrath is neglected by many millennial writers. The attempts to make it fit an event in history such as the destruction of the Temple in AD 70 or to spread it throughout history dilutes the impact of God's wrath. We have seen, if we connect the relevant Old Testament prophecies concerning *the day of the Lord* with the events in Revelation, that history is reaching a climax prior to the return of Christ. This is why these passages are called *apocalyptic.* They are pointing to a future time of doom and disaster. However bad history has been, and it must have seemed apocalyptic at times to the people involved, it has not yet reached the climax described as *the day of the Lord.*

Events in Revelation

We shall now examine some of the events unleashed in Revelation by the wrath of God. I do not propose to attempt a detailed review; but rather I shall attempt to give the reader an idea of how it unfolds. There is much symbolism in Revelation, but this still does not mean that one has to resort to widely different interpretations. I explain the way I understand scripture in Chapter 7. I try to stick to the literal meaning unless it is impossible to do so. Even when the author is using a metaphor, as he often does in Revelation, it is still reasonable to believe that actual events are being described.

The other aspect of Revelation which needs some explanation is the time sequence. I am inclined to accept the view of most theologians that Revelation is not entirely sequential. God's wrath unfolds through three sets of seven events: the breaking of seven seals, the blowing of seven trumpets (woes) and the pouring out of seven bowls (vials). Each of the trumpet and bowl judgements may be sequential, but the first four seals, better known as the four *Horsemen of the Apocalypse*, may represent the backdrop in which the remaining judgements unfold.

The apostle John experiences his vision as happening in both heaven and earth. In heaven we see the judgements of God expressing his wrath; these are administered by angels. We then see the consequences of each judgement as it appears on earth. The angels appear to operate in both the natural and the spiritual realm. They operate directly on nature to cause natural disasters, but they also release satanic spirits to wreak havoc and destruction on earth through human conflict. We see this satanic activity clearly in trumpet judgements 5 and 6 and bowl judgement 6, (*Revelation 9:1-11; 9:13-17; 16:12-16*).

The seven seals (Revelation Chapter 6)

The seals are opened first. The first four, the four *Horsemen of the Apocalypse*, seem to represent the panorama of events in which God's judgements take place. The first two horses, white and red, represent warfare and the destruction of war. The white horse indicates the conquering of nations by more powerful nations, while the red horse represents the death and destruction that follow these wars. There is an absence of peace during this time. The third or black horse suggests severe shortages of food, while the fourth or pale horse represents death which kills up to a quarter of the earth's population through war, famine and disease (*Revelation 6:1-8*). The four *Horsemen of the Apocalypse* have caught the imagination of the human race throughout history. They have been the subject of art, literature and more recently films. They represent an appropriate backdrop to the judgements and suffering of the Tribulation.

The trumpet judgements (Revelation Chapters 8 and 9)

The first four trumpet judgements (*Revelation 8:7-12*) suggest destruction through man-made or natural events. The first trumpet leads to a burning of a third of the earth. Could this be the devastation wrought by nuclear war? The apostle John could not possibly have known about nuclear war in his day – all he could see were the consequences of such a war on the natural world.

The second trumpet is interesting because it could be describing a literal event that some geologists and volcanologists now talk about as a certainty – the only issue is when. This was not surmised until the twentieth century. This event is the predicted landslip of half of the island of La Palma in the Canary Islands. The island sits on a geological fault and is extremely unstable.[4] If half the island slips into the Atlantic Ocean, it could generate a mega tsunami which might inundate the Atlantic coast of Europe, Africa, and North and South America with great destruction. This may not be the meaning of the second trumpet, but the geological instability of La Palma presents a realistic realisation in the natural world of this trumpet judgement.

The third trumpet sounds like the effect of an asteroid falling to earth, an event that is considered much more likely than it used to be, now that modern astronomy has revealed the paths of asteroids leaving the asteroid belt between Mars and Jupiter. Asteroids and large meteorites do not have to be very large to cause immense damage. The reason for this is their velocity and the fact that friction with the atmosphere may heat them up so that they explode while still in the air. The devastation caused by a small asteroid hitting Tunguska, a remote region of Siberia, in 1908 is a reminder of this. The shock wave from the atmospheric explosion flattened the trees for miles around.

The fourth trumpet describes a partial darkening of light from the sun, moon and stars. This could arise naturally from volcanic eruptions as has been known to happen in history[5] or it could arise from all the debris thrust into the air through a nuclear war, sometimes described as 'nuclear winter'. Its effects are not as severe as the darkness described under Seal six which arises from what must be a massive earthquake (*Revelation 6:12-13*).

The fifth and sixth trumpet judgements move from the natural realm into the spiritual. Both judgements, and in particular the fifth trumpet, are described in symbolic language. Trumpet five would seem to be about demonic activity directed towards the human race. 'Locusts' (demons)[6] are released from a place which Scripture calls the *abyss* or *bottomless pit* and given power to torment people, but not to kill them. Their leader is named as Abaddon, the fallen angel in charge of the abyss.

Trumpet six, however, suggests human warfare. 200 million troops[7] in the Middle East are empowered by four satanic angels who are released from being bound near the River Euphrates. (The fact that they are bound and released by an angel from God suggests they are fallen or satanic angels.) The destruction from this conflict must be enormous as it is one of the judgements leading to the death of one third of humanity.

The bowl judgements (Revelation Chapters 15 and 16)
The first five bowls (also called plagues) would seem to be natural events carried out directly by God's angels. We are not told what it means when the sea becomes like the blood of a corpse (Bowl 2) or that the fresh water of rivers and springs becomes blood (Bowl 3), only that the consequences are severe. With the sixth bowl we have another example of God's angel releasing demonic spirits. They go forth to entice the kings of the world to assemble for battle on *"the great day of God the almighty"* at a place called Armageddon (*Revelation 16:12-16*).

God's wrath is finished with the seventh bowl (*Revelation 15:1; 16:17-20*). This leads to a huge, worldwide earthquake with topographical effects on the earth and a major impact on Jerusalem:

> ... *a great earthquake such as there had never been since man was on the earth, so great was that earthquake. The great city was split into three parts, and the cities of the nations fell... And every island fled away, and no mountains were to be found. And great hailstones, about one hundred pounds each, fell from heaven on people...*
>
> (Revelation 16:18-20)

The consequences of this earthquake on Jerusalem are described in *Zechariah 14* and *Ezekiel 47*. Near or on the very day of the Lord's return, the Mount of Olives is split in two from east to west. One of the consequences is that fresh water will flow from Jerusalem into the Dead Sea to transform it so that fish can live there (*Ezekiel 47:8-10*).

The impact of these and other judgements in a short space of time, namely seven years, will be unimaginable. I have described most, but not all of the events happening under the three sets of judgements. It is interesting to note that at several points in Revelation, human beings refuse to repent and even curse God, despite their suffering (see *Revelation 9:20-21; 16:8-9, 11* and *21*).

Conclusion

In the second half of this chapter I have attempted to explain some of the events described in Revelation as literally as possible. If we do not accept this literal approach and try to explain the narrative as a metaphor, we are still faced with the vivid expression of God's wrath. There is no way we can make a metaphor or symbol of such statements as these:

◊   The wrath of the Lamb, for the great day of their wrath has come. (*Revelation 6:16-17*)

◊   The seven golden bowls full of the wrath of God. (*Revelation 15:7*)

◊   For with them the wrath of God is finished. (*Revelation 15:1*)

The consequences of God's wrath and the harm done by the Antichrist prior to the immediate return of Christ are overwhelming. Jesus himself warned that unless God brings this time to a close, no human life would remain on earth (*Matthew 24:21-22*). I think, and I quite understand why, that many writers on the end-times have not faced up to this decimation of the world's population through the outpouring of God's wrath and the activities of Satan.

NOTES

1. There is a third time when God displays his wrath, and mercifully for us this is not vented on the human race, but on the Lord Jesus Christ on the Cross. This was God's anger at the sum total of human sins, the punishment for which was taken by Jesus. We cannot comprehend what he went through on the Cross and during his descent into hell, though certain passages in Scripture hint at it. (See *Isaiah 52:13 – 53:12*; *Psalm 22* and *Psalm 88*). However, we do have to receive the release from this punishment by accepting what Jesus has done for us and repenting of our sins. To refuse this is to remain under God's wrath and his future judgement and punishment.

2. We should certainly not play down the decimation of the pandemics in history in order to emphasize the coming trouble in the Tribulation.

   The Justinian plague was a devastating epidemic that may have started in Egypt in AD 541 and which spread to Constantinople, Persia and southern Europe. It arose during the reign of Justinian, the emperor of the Eastern Roman Empire (Byzantium). It flared up, on and off, for the next two centuries. Although population statistics are not reliable for this time, it is clear from contemporary accounts that the death toll was enormous, perhaps between 10 and 20 million in places around the Mediterranean. Many people died from starvation because farmers were dying from the plague.

   Like the Justinian plague, the Black Death was a pandemic of bubonic plague, this time in the fourteenth century. It spread throughout Europe and Russia starting in 1347. The death toll was huge. It is estimated that 20 million people died in Europe in the plague's first five years, equivalent to about one third of the population. Many cities lost more than this. The impact on the medieval economy was enormous. In England numerous villages ceased to exist. Labouring men were scarce and the medieval system of feudal servitude began to give way to the capitalist hiring of labour.

3. It should be said that some writers see a two-fold application of *the day of the Lord* in the Old Testament, meaning both the near future and the distant future. While this is true of some Old Testament prophecy, I find this difficult to accept for *the day of the Lord*. *Zephaniah 1:14-18* gives a most solemn description of this day and applies it to the whole of mankind, suggesting that God will destroy the inhabitants of the earth. This is echoed by Jesus in *Matthew 24:21-22* where he says people will only survive because the days are cut short. Zephaniah was a prophet to the nation of Judah. I cannot see how these words could apply to the coming exile of Judah to Babylon and the destruction of Solomon's Temple in 586 BC, or the more distant destruction of the Second Temple in AD 70, terrible as these were. I can only see Zephaniah's words applying to the Tribulation.

4. There are numerous articles on the Internet about the potential landslip of the island of La Palma through the activities of its volcano, Cumbre Vieja, and the likely consequences of such a landslip. There are also articles on mega tsunamis. It is only fair to mention that some scientists dispute the predictions of the pessimists. They argue that the tsunami from a landslip

would not be as damaging as one from an underwater earthquake. However, Christians need to be aware that the Bible's vivid statement: *"Something like a great mountain, burning with fire, was thrown into the sea..."* (*Revelation 8:8-9*), could certainly match the landslip of the island of La Palma, were this to happen. What the rest of the verse means when it says, *"a third of the sea became blood"* is not made clear.

5.   The Internet has articles on the varied atmospheric effects of volcanic eruptions, one of the most dramatic in recent history being the eruption of the island of Krakatoa in Indonesia in 1883. An informative article on the climatic effects of historic eruptions occurs on the website of the American Museum of Natural History:

<http://www.amnh.org/education/resources/rfl/web/bulletins/earth/A/1/2/index.html>

6.   The text makes clear that these are not ordinary locusts. They are malevolent, intelligent spirit beings capable of taking orders from their leader, who have previously been confined to a place called the abyss or the bottomless pit (see *Luke 8:31; Revelation 9:11*).

7.   There is no reason provided in the text for not taking the number, "twice ten thousand times ten thousand" literally. The apostle John himself says, "I heard their number".

5 *THE RAPTURE AND ITS TIMING*

The Rapture is an event clearly described in two New Testament scriptures and implied in others. Let us first examine the apostle Paul's words in *1 Thessalonians* and *1 Corinthians*:

> *For this we declare to you by a word from the Lord, that we who are alive, who are left until the coming of the Lord, will not precede those who have fallen asleep. For the Lord himself will descend from heaven with a cry of command, with the voice of an archangel, and with the sound of the trumpet of God. And the dead in Christ will rise first. Then we who are alive, who are left, will be caught up together with them in the clouds to meet the Lord in the air, and so we will always be with the Lord.*
>
> (1 Thessalonians 4:15-17)

> *Behold! I tell you a mystery. We shall not all sleep, but we shall all be changed, in a moment, in the twinkling of an eye, at the last trumpet. For the trumpet will sound, and the dead will be raised imperishable, and we shall be changed. For this perishable body must put on the imperishable, and this mortal body must put on immortality.*
>
> (1 Corinthians 15:51-53)

By way of explanation: the word 'sleep' is sometimes used by Paul to mean physical death while the soul and spirit wait for the resurrection of the body. The Greek word used for 'caught up' in the first passage of scripture is the Greek word '*harpazo*' and we meet it later in another relevant scripture.

These passages clearly teach that a generation of Christians will avoid death. They will be transformed rather than resurrected.

It would seem too that Jesus is referring to this Rapture in his Olivet discourse. In Matthew he says:

> But concerning that day and hour no one knows, not even the angels of heaven, nor the Son, but the Father only.
>
> *(Matthew 24:36)*

> So will be the coming of the Son of Man. Then two men will be in the field; one will be taken and one left. Two women will be grinding at the mill; one will be taken and one left. Therefore, stay awake, for you do not know on what day your Lord is coming.
>
> *(Matthew 24:39-42)*

In Luke Jesus adds these words:[1]

> I tell you, in that night there will be two in one bed. One will be taken and the other left.
>
> *(Luke 17:34)*

Less convincingly in my view, some writers offer the beginning of *John Chapter 14* as evidence for the Rapture. Here, Jesus tells his disciples that he goes to prepare a place for them in his Father's house and that he will come again to collect them (*John 14:1-3*).

When we first learn about the Rapture it may seem to us like a very bizarre event. We are envisaging millions of Christians mysteriously leaving the earth in a moment of time, leaving non-believers wondering what has happened and where they have all gone. Popular premillennialist writers envisage nerve-racking scenarios with many cars, engines or aircraft being left driverless. I suspect the bizarreness of what is known as the Pre-tribulation Rapture is what has led some theologians to consider the Rapture as a much less dramatic event. They believe that those Christians who are still alive will meet Christ at the end of the Tribulation when the dead in Christ are resurrected and the living receive their new, incorruptible bodies. We will examine the pros and cons of the alternative views when considering the timing of the Rapture in the next chapter. The two major positions are: the *pre-tribulation* and the *post-tribulation* raptures, along with two lesser known views, the *mid-tribulation* and *pre-wrath* raptures.

Biblical precedent for the Rapture

Although it may seem a bizarre event, the Rapture is not without precedent in the Bible, although on a much smaller scale. We know from Scripture that both Enoch and Elijah were taken up to heaven without experiencing physical death (*Genesis 5:21-24* and *2 Kings 2:1-12*). On another occasion, this time in the New Testament, the evangelist Philip was led to speak to the Ethiopian eunuch about the good news of Jesus. Immediately after his conversation Philip was supernaturally carried away by the Holy Spirit and found himself in another town, Azotus. (The Greek word *harpazo* used to describe the Rapture in *1 Thessalonians*, is also used to describe Philip's supernatural transport in *Acts 8:26-40*).

The other point to make is that if we believe that Christ is returning to the earth, and most Christians do, then there will be a generation of believers who do not experience death. This is a logical conclusion. Those of us alive when Jesus returns, whether secretly before the Tribulation or very publicly at the end of it, will meet him and receive our transformed bodies ready for eternity. I do not think any believer expects Christ to greet them in person and then require them to die so that they can be resurrected!

Supporters of a Pre-tribulation Rapture think that believers will be removed from earth, be transformed and transported to heaven and then take part as the Bride in the Marriage to the Lamb (the Lord Jesus). This will happen while the Tribulation is running its course back on earth. The reasoning appears to be that the Marriage Supper of the Lamb is described in *Revelation 19:6-8*, before Christ returns to earth to dispose of the Antichrist, the false prophet and the armies arrayed against him (*Revelation 19:11-21*). The next mention of the Bride of Christ is in *Revelation 21:9-10*.

I think we have to be very careful here. *Revelation 21* is describing the new heaven and earth which occur after all the earthly events described in Revelation, including the Millennium (if there is indeed a literal 1000-year reign of Christ on earth). By this stage the Church will be complete. It will include all the Old Testament saints, all the Jewish and Gentile saints of the Church age, the people saved during the Tribulation, and those saved during the Millennium. The belief that the Marriage of the Bride to the Lamb takes place immediately after the Rapture and before the Church is complete, is at best supposition. The logical view is that the marriage will happen when the Bride of Christ is complete. It does mean that we have to be careful when we take the prophecies of Revelation sequentially. There are some clear sequences, but others are not so certain.

The timing of the Rapture

All Christians, whatever their view of the Tribulation and the Millennium, believe that Jesus Christ is coming back for his Church.[2] They may not think he is coming back to reveal himself to Israel and they may not believe that the Tribulation is a seven-year period of intense trial for the inhabitants of the earth. They may believe that the Tribulation spans the time of Church history (amillennialists), with evil increasing in intensity prior to the Lord's return, or they may think (postmillennialists) that the world will gradually improve as more and more people are won for Christ. These postmillennialists believe that it is the Church's job to make the world a suitable place for the King's return. For amillennialists and postmillennialists the Rapture will occur when Christ physically returns to earth itself – that generation which is still alive will be caught up to meet him. The Great White Throne judgement (*Revelation 20:11-12*) will take place, our eternal destinies will be confirmed and the new heaven and earth will be created, all in a very short space of time following Christ's return.

The timing of the Rapture is only really an issue for the premillennialists who envisage a specific seven-year span for the Tribulation.

Some considerations

In a later chapter we shall review the different millennial positions. For the moment let us assume that the reader has been persuaded that the premillennial position is the correct approach to the end-times and the return of Christ. This is probably the most popular view among ordinary evangelical Christians and is also held by many theologians.

The question then is whether one believes in a pre-tribulation or a post-tribulation rapture.[3] Let me make clear straight away that however passionately one subscribes to a particular view there is not a conclusive answer to this question. At the end of the debate it is a matter of the balance of evidence. One can do a Google search on the Internet on the two approaches to the Rapture and see titles such as:

16 Proofs for a pre-tribulation rapture

4 Proofs for a post-tribulation rapture etc

Proofs imply certainty and these are not certainties. At best they are evidence and in the end evidence has to be weighed. Whereas I think we can establish from Scripture the certainty of the return of the Jews to their ancient land,[4] I do not think we can do the same for the timing of the Rapture. To arrive at certain theological positions we sometimes find that Christians will ignore scriptures or spiritualize them to change their literal meaning. However, that is not the case among the serious contenders in this debate. They use rational arguments when assessing the scriptures to arrive at their positions. Thus we cannot prove one position over the other, but we can weigh the evidence. We may conclude that the evidence favours one view rather than another or we may decide that the evidence is too evenly balanced to reach a conclusion.

Is the debate important?

In my view it is very important. Some writers play down the significance of the time of the Rapture saying that what really matters is that Christ is returning for his Church and we should rejoice in that fact. No one will want to disagree with this sentiment, but the manner in which we meet him is highly significant and very different in the two scenarios. In the pre-tribulation rapture the Church misses the Tribulation and in the post-tribulation rapture the Church goes through it. If we are alive as the time for Christ's return approaches, then we ought to be concerned. We need to be prepared for both scenarios; otherwise we may find ourselves caught unawares like the unbelieving world.

If the Church goes through the Tribulation there can be no doubt that many Christians will lose their lives. The world's population[5] will be greatly reduced and like unbelievers Christians will suffer in the natural and man-made disasters that happen during this time. Furthermore, among those who survive these disasters many will be pursued by the Antichrist who will target both Jews and Christians. Some writers take comfort in the protection given to the 'woman' in *Revelation Chapter 12* who escapes to the wilderness and is given supernatural protection, but as I stated in Chapter 3 this woman must represent the Jewish nation (or part of it) gathered in Israel. It is unrealistic to think that the 'woman' is the worldwide Church which is protected across the world in more than one wilderness. Not only that, but later in the chapter it is said that the dragon (the devil) goes off to make war on those who keep God's commandments and hold to the testimony of Jesus. Such people really are the Church, either because it goes through the Tribulation, or because these are converts to Christianity made during this time.

The persecuted Church

Having said this, it is also important to realize that many Christians through the ages have experienced their own tribulation ending in martyrdom. For them it would not have mattered whether the Rapture was before or after the Tribulation. Any attempt to favour the pre-tribulation Rapture on the grounds that we will escape persecution is a mistaken one. David Pawson who comes down on the side of the Rapture following the Tribulation, quotes from the writings of Corrie ten Boom, the famous Dutch Christian evangelist:

> *I have been in countries where the saints are already suffering terrible persecution. In China the Christians were told: 'Don't worry, before the tribulation comes, you will be translated, raptured.' Then came a terrible persecution. Millions of Christians were tortured to death. Later I heard a bishop from China say, sadly: 'We have failed. We should have made the people strong for persecution rather than telling them Jesus would come first. Turning to me, he said: 'Tell the people how to be strong in times of persecution, how to stand when the tribulation comes – to stand and not faint.' I feel I have a divine mandate to go and tell the people of this world that it is possible to be strong in the Lord Jesus Christ. We are in training for the tribulation.[6]*

What this timely quotation tells me is that we must weigh the evidence in as objective a manner as possible. We only have to look at various parts of the world today, places such as Nigeria, Syria and Iraq to see that many Christians are being persecuted and even martyred for their faith. It is not surprising if these Christians think the Tribulation is almost upon us.

Conclusion

The timing of the Rapture is a pre-occupation of the Church. Most Jews and unbelieving Gentiles have probably never heard of it. The Tribulation is about God's dealings with an unrepentant world which may or may not concern believers. Christians who come to faith during this time will clearly be caught up in it. Those who are believers before this time may or may not be involved and this will depend on the timing of the Rapture. This is the significance of the pre- or post-tribulation rapture positions.

In the next chapter we will weigh the evidence for the pre- and post-tribulation views of the Rapture and make passing reference to the mid-tribulation and pre-wrath points of view.

NOTES

1. Some writers put the opposite view on these verses. They say it does not apply to the Rapture, but to the Lord's return to earth. They argue that those taken represent the unbelievers while the believers are left. Their reasoning is that in the days of Noah it was the sinners who were taken (swept away in the flood), not the righteous.

    It is difficult to see the logic in this view. The text describes a sudden and unexpected arrival to meet with people in civilian activities such as working in a field, grinding corn or sleeping in bed. This is very different from the Lord's arrival on earth in the midst of the battle of Armageddon where he vanquishes the Antichrist. If it is the sinners who are taken, then what happens to them? There is no indication of sudden destruction of civilians at Jesus' arrival. Those who are killed are the soldiers under the Antichrist. The judgement of the sheep and goat nations happens after Jesus' return.

    It seems more likely to me that the parallel with Noah's Flood is the sudden, unexpected return of the Lord, and not with the people who are taken on this occasion.

2. Some believers, for example some preterists, hold the view that Jesus' return is spiritual and not physical.

3. I shall also make mention of the mid-tribulation and pre-wrath positions in the next chapter.

4. See my book: *Has God really finished with Israel?*

5. The present world population is 7.3 billion (March 2015).

6. David Pawson, *When Jesus Returns,* P. 199.

6 *PRE- OR POST- TRIBULATION RAPTURE?*

We ended Chapter 5 with the issue of a marked difference of opinion among Christians and theologians as to when the Rapture takes place. Those who consider that it occurs prior to the Tribulation are called pre-tribulationists while those who think that it occurs at the end of the Tribulation, just prior to Christ's return, are known as post-tribulationists. There are two further groups with a much smaller following who believe that the Rapture occurs within the Tribulation. These subscribe either to the mid-tribulation rapture or to the pre-wrath rapture.

For most of my forty years as a Christian I have believed in the pre-tribulation rapture. If I am honest about it, this belief has contained an element of comfort, namely that if I am living in the end-times I will not have to go through this terrible time. Now that I have done the research for the book I am no longer so certain. What I do know is that an emotional approach, however understandable, will not help us to weigh the evidence. This is also true of the opposite position whereby some believers think it is necessary for the Church to be refined by going through the Tribulation. This view overlooks the fact that most believers have died throughout history in various states of sanctification, and that only a proportion of the believers in Christ would experience the particular refining of the Tribulation.

We are now going to examine the evidence for the different positions, especially the first two. This requirement to weigh the evidence may disappoint Christians, who have put their faith in a pre-tribulation rapture, but I think it is realistic in the light of the scriptures.

It will help the reader to have the relevant scriptures to hand when we consider the Rapture. I would consider these to be the most important:

Matthew Chapters 24 and *25*

Luke 12:35-48; 17:20-37; 21:10-28 and *34-36*

1 Corinthians 15:51-53

1 Thessalonians 4:15-17

2 Thessalonians 2:1-12

Evidence for a pre-tribulation Rapture

This is the view that believers will not go through the Tribulation, except for those who convert to Christ during this tumultuous time.

1. The Tribulation: Israel and the Jews are centre-stage

The evidence for this is striking. In Chapter 3 I listed eight reasons why the mid-section of Revelation (*Revelation Chapters 4 to 18*) is about Israel and not about the Church on earth. (There are certainly references to the saints in heaven.) This is in keeping with all the Old Testament prophecies concerning the restoration of Israel. It does not mean that the Church is unimportant; it simply means its work on earth during the Church age is largely or completely done. Unbelievers, both Jewish and Gentile, will join the Church during the Tribulation and many will be martyred. There is reason to think that evangelism will principally be the work of Jewish converts, perhaps the 144,000 Jewish males who are sealed for service in *Revelation Chapter 7*. (*Isaiah 66:19* is a possible pointer to such evangelism.)

2. Is the return of Christ a single event or could it happen in two stages?

We need to examine the evidence as to whether the return of Christ is a single event or whether it could occur in two phases with an interval of indeterminate length. The first phase would be a return for his saints in the Rapture and this would be invisible to the world, (though its consequences would certainly be felt). The second phase would be a very visible return to the earth – in what is usually known as the Return or Second Advent of Jesus Christ. Those who subscribe to a pre-tribulation rapture believe that Jesus' return happens in two stages.

The most common objection to the idea of a two-stage return of Christ, with the Rapture preceding the Tribulation, is that Scripture does not describe such a return. However, examination of Jesus' own words in the Olivet discourse (*Matthew Chapters 24* and *25; Luke Chapters 17* and *21*) suggest that we need to take a more nuanced approach. Some verses clearly conflict with the idea of a single event:

> *Immediately after the tribulation of those days the sun will be darkened, and the moon will not give its light, and the stars will fall from heaven, and the powers of the heavens will be shaken. Then will appear in heaven the sign of the Son of Man, and then all the tribes of the earth will mourn, and they will see the Son of Man coming on the clouds of heaven with power and great glory.*
>
> (Matthew 24:29-30)

This conflicts with the passage a little later in the chapter:

> *But concerning that day and hour no one knows, not even the angels of heaven, nor the Son, but the Father only. For as were the days of Noah, so will be the coming of the Son of Man. For as in those days before the flood they were eating and drinking, marrying and giving in marriage, until the day when Noah entered the ark, and they were unaware until the flood came and swept them all away, so will be the coming of the Son of Man. Then two men will be in the field; one will be taken and one left. Two women will be grinding at the mill; one will be taken and one left. Therefore, stay awake, for you do not know on what day your Lord is coming... Therefore you also must be ready, for the Son of Man is coming at an hour you do not expect.*
>
> (Matthew 24:36-44)

The second passage is thought by many believers to refer to the Rapture while the first clearly refers to the visible return of Christ to earth.

There are several observations to be made about these passages which suggest that they do not describe the same event in time. The first passage describes a very visible return of the Son of Man at the **end** of the Tribulation coming in great power and glory. The equivalent passage in Luke (*Luke 21:25-27*) makes it absolutely clear that people will be aware of this event. They will be living in a time of stress and will faint with fear at what is coming on the earth. If we Christians do live through the Tribulation we shall know with the certainty of Scripture that Christ will return at the end of it. Furthermore, we shall be very aware of the return when it happens.[1]

The second passage contrasts sharply with this very visible appearance. It speaks of surprise at the Lord's coming when even believers are not expecting him. It compares the time with the days of Noah when everyone was carrying on as normal except for Noah and his family who prepared for and warned about the coming flood. No doubt Noah warned people about the coming Flood, and was duly mocked for it. The passage warns us to be ready for an unexpected coming – we are told that it will happen, but not when.

The passage goes on to describe a strange event (*verse 40*); people will be occupied with their daily activities and suddenly some of them will disappear. Of two men working in a field, one will be taken and the other left. The same will apply to two women working at a mill. In *Luke 17:34* it refers to two sleeping in bed; one will be taken and the other left. These verses suggest that this surprise event will happen simultaneously across the world. The implication is that believers will be taken and unbelievers will be left behind. The whole thrust of the Matthew passage is that we need to be aware and we need to be ready for an unexpected event.[2]

There is a further point in this passage (*Matthew 24:36-44*) which lends credence to the separation of the Rapture from Jesus' return to earth. Just prior to the Rapture conditions on earth will be **normal**. The days are compared to those of Noah, when people were carrying on with everyday activities. No one apart from Noah and his family was aware (or had taken notice of Noah's warnings) that disaster was imminent. So it will be with the Rapture – it will happen unexpectedly. The world at large will not expect the Rapture and if they have heard of it from their believing friends, they will have dismissed it. In sharp contrast this cannot possibly be said about the time prior to Jesus' return. The world in the Tribulation will be anything but normal.

The parable of the ten virgins follows this passage in *Matthew Chapter 25*. It may simply be a parable on the need to be ready, although it may possibly be an apt description of what happens at the Rapture.[3] The gospel writer closes with the words:

> *Watch therefore, for you know neither the day nor the hour [when the Bridegroom returns].*
>
> *(Matthew 25:13)* [comment added]

This element of surprise will not exist, at least for the Christians, once the Antichrist has appeared and the Tribulation is under way. If our understanding of the prophet Daniel's 70 weeks is correct, then we shall indeed know the likely date for Christ's visible return.

When we come to the apostle Paul's discourse on the Rapture (see the start of the previous chapter), we find some sense of surprise, that we shall suddenly find ourselves transformed and meeting the Lord in the air. It seems logically unlikely that this will happen during the Lord's return to earth at his Second Advent, where the Bible says that every eye shall see him. Such a step would require believers alive on earth to be transformed, to meet the Lord in the air and then to return back down to earth as soon as this has happened.[4] It seems unlikely that raptured believers will return immediately to the carnage of the Tribulation from which they have just been rescued.

The popular premillennial view is that the Rapture will happen at some undisclosed point prior to the beginning of the Tribulation which, when it happens lasts for seven years and is brought to an end by the physical return of Jesus Christ to the Mount of Olives in Jerusalem (see *Acts 1:9-11; Zechariah 14:4*). This view offers no indication of whether the Rapture occurs immediately before or well in advance of the Tribulation.

3. The wrath of God

As we have seen the Tribulation is an exceptional time on earth. It is one of only two times when the whole human race is directly subject to God's wrath. For most of history the human race has been subject to the consequences of the Fall of Man, to human sin and to the malice of Satan. The evil consequences of these things have been allowed by

God, but not directly administered by him. Individuals and even groups of people have experienced God's wrath; we see that particularly with the Israelites and in local situations such as the destruction of Sodom, but the human race as a whole has not experienced this wrath except at the time of the Noahic flood. Such direct wrath from God will appear again during the Tribulation. There are many verses which speak of the wrath of God, but it is only when we get to Revelation that the pouring out of this wrath is revealed (see *Revelation 6:16-17; 14:10 and 19; 15:1; 16:1 and 19; 19:15*). This is not the storing up of God's wrath to be revealed at the final judgement (*Revelation 20:11-15*) but the outworking of God's fury on a sinful and rebellious human race. The frequency of the word 'wrath' from *Revelation Chapter 6* onwards makes clear that the Tribulation is a time of unprecedented trouble on earth.

A number of scriptures make it clear that believers are not destined for the wrath of God. They may suffer at the hands of evil men and through the hatred of Satan, even to the point of death, but they will not experience God's wrath. The whole point of Jesus' death on the Cross was that he should feel the full force of God's anger and righteous judgement in our place, so that we could be spared and be clothed with his righteousness. God's pent-up anger is poured out at the end of an age in which he has displayed patience and mercy on those who have ignored his offer of salvation and gone deeper into sin through alignment with the works of Satan.

The apostle Paul says immediately after talking about the Rapture and *the day of the Lord*:

> *For God has not destined us for wrath, but to obtain salvation through our Lord Jesus Christ...*
>
> (1 Thessalonians 5:9)

Jesus says during the Olivet discourse, when he is talking about both the destruction of Jerusalem (AD 70) and the last days:

> *Watch therefore, and pray always that you may be counted worthy to escape all these things that will come to pass...*
>
> (Luke 21:36 NKJV)

Again the risen Christ says to the Church at Philadelphia:

Because you have kept my word about patient endurance, I will keep you from the hour of trial that is coming on the whole world, to try those who dwell on the earth.

(Revelation 3:10)

It is generally agreed by theologians that the seven churches of Asia Minor not only represented seven individual churches, but types of the Church down the ages. Philadelphia and Smyrna were the two completely faithful churches with whom Christ found no fault. Smyrna represented the persecuted Church, whose testing would experience the malevolence of Satan, down the ages. We are not told whether the church of Philadelphia will escape the evil attentions of Satan, but we are told that it will escape a worldwide tribulation on account of its faithfulness. The clear implications from these two faithful churches is that the Church suffers at the hands of evil men and Satan, even to the point of martyrdom, but NOT from the direct wrath of God.

In sombre contrast the church of Laodicea is given no such comfort. They are counselled to buy gold refined by fire. Could this mean that they may go through the Tribulation, being refined in the process? The famous verse: *"Behold, I stand at the door and knock..."* (*Revelation 3:20*) spoken by Jesus at the end of his rebuke to the Laodiceans suggests that he wants to come into their lives either for salvation or to renew his relationship with Christians who were once alive to him. The message to the Laodicean church makes sober reading. Why would Jesus warn us in the Olivet discourse to watch, stay awake and pray, if it were not possible to avoid the Tribulation? However, the condition is that we must be ready for him.

There is a further argument which warrants consideration. Abraham's nephew Lot is spared the destruction of Sodom and Gomorrah as a result of Abraham's intercession (*Genesis Chapters 18 and 19*). One of the interesting things about this passage is the way Abraham approaches God. He is very concerned about the fate of the righteous people living in Sodom. He asks God to spare the city if he can find fifty righteous people living there. As God agrees to his request Abraham gradually whittles this number down to ten, but that is still not enough to save the city. Only righteous Lot (*2 Peter 2:7*) and his immediate family are deemed worthy of deliverance. His two prospective sons-in-law thought Lot was jesting and his wife looked back, so that only Lot and his two daughters were saved. Lot and his family had to be forcibly removed by the angels before the Lord's judgement fell (*Genesis 19:15*). In verse 22 the angel tells Lot; *"Escape there quickly, for I can do nothing till you arrive there."* (at the village of Zoar away from Sodom).

The conclusion that supporters of a pre-tribulation rapture draw from this story, is that God removes the righteous (the believing Church) before he can judge the unbelieving world during the Tribulation. This judgement of wrath is quite different from the suffering and persecution experienced by Christians at the hands of Satan and evil men. To let us go through this judgement would be to judge us a second time. If our sins are truly judged in Christ we have been made righteous in him, and God cannot judge us a second time.

This principle was true of Noah at the time of the Flood and of Lot at the time of Sodom and Gomorrah. The righteous men and their immediate families were removed before the judgement. It is a powerful argument for believing that the Church will be removed prior to the judgement of the Tribulation.

Many premillennial supporters of a post-tribulation rapture also agree that born-again believers are not destined to receive God's wrath. They tend to see Christians being protected through the Tribulation, rather than taken out of it. However, the extent of the destruction (as detailed in Chapter 4) makes the idea of protection difficult to sustain.

4. Restraining the Antichrist

There is a further major consideration which suggests that the Rapture may precede the Tribulation. The apostle Paul talks specifically about the Antichrist as '*the man of lawlessness*' in *2 Thessalonians Chapter 2*. He first makes clear that *the day of the Lord* will not come:

> ... *unless the rebellion comes first, and the man of lawlessness is revealed, the son of destruction, who opposes and exalts himself against every so-called god or object of worship...*
>
> *(2 Thessalonians 2:3-4)*

Paul then goes on to reveal that something is restraining the appearance of this evil man (*2 Thessalonians 2:6-8*). The Antichrist cannot be revealed until this restraint is removed. Paul implies that his readers know the identity of this restraint, but it is not spelt out. Writers have tended to identify this restraint either as the Holy Spirit or the Church or even human governments. I do not think that governments which are becoming increasingly godless in their behaviour are serious candidates. This restraint must be spiritual in nature so let us consider the first two suggestions. Neither agent alone satisfies this restraint. Clearly the Holy Spirit is not removed from earth at any point, but the Church *in itself* does not have the inherent power to prevent the appearance of the Antichrist. However, if we say that the restraint is the Holy Spirit operating through believers in Christ, in other words through the Church as a whole, then its identity is clear. If the Church is removed through the Rapture, then all those believers whose righteousness in Christ and whose prayer life helps to inhibit evil on earth, will no longer be there to check the activities of Satan. The Antichrist can now be revealed. The Holy Spirit still perceives all that happens on earth, but he is not called upon to hold back evil in the absence of millions of believing Christians who are now with the Lord in heaven. As Hosea says, the Lord has withdrawn himself (*Hosea 5:6*).

5. Christ's warnings to be prepared

The thread running through Jesus' Olivet discourse is that his followers should be very prepared for his return (*Matthew 24:42, 44; 25:13; Luke 21:34-36*). They should not relax their guard, be caught unawares as the world was at the time of Noah or be deceived by false prophets. The Lord will come like a thief in the night. It should be noted that once the Antichrist has appeared and the Tribulation gets under way the element of surprise (*Matthew 25:13*) would be lost. If the Tribulation lasts seven years, as argued in this book, then we shall know the time of Christ's arrival.

Furthermore, in *Luke 21:36* Christ specifically warns us to be watchful and pray that we may avoid this time of trouble. My interlinear Greek-English New Testament translates this verse as follows:[5]

> But be ye watchful at every time **begging** that ye may be able
> to **escape** these things all being about to happen, and to
> stand before the Son of Man.
>
> [emphasis added]

Some writers argue that being 'kept from the hour of trial' (*Revelation 3:10*) could mean that the Lord will protect people in the time of trial rather than remove them from it. This is difficult to square with the fact that Revelation speaks of so many being martyred during the Tribulation. Verses quoted earlier (*1 Thessalonians 5:9*; *Luke 21:35-36* and *Revelation 3:10*) were spoken to Christians prior to the time of tribulation. They are much more likely to mean that the Church existing prior to the Tribulation will avoid these events.

Evidence for a post-tribulation Rapture

We will now review the evidence for the opposing opinion that the Church does go through the time of trouble known as the Tribulation. As in the previous section I am simply asking the reader to reflect on the kind of arguments used by supporters of a particular point of view. I am not necessarily expressing my agreement with them.

Some Christians have difficulty with the idea of large numbers of believers suddenly being removed from the earth and its impact on an astonished world. It is indeed a strange idea to contemplate, but it does not really constitute an objection to a pre-tribulation rapture. As we have seen, the scriptures clearly state that those alive at the time will be caught up to meet the Lord in the air (*1 Thessalonians 4:16-17*). It may seem less strange if it happens at the close of the Tribulation chaos, but that is not a scriptural reason for arguing that it must therefore do so.

1. Why should the Church avoid the martyrdom of the Tribulation?

This is a powerful argument against a pre-tribulation rapture. It asks why the particular group of Christians constituting the Church prior to the Tribulation should escape the suffering and martyrdom of this period when so many Christians have been martyred in history and are still being martyred today, and converts during the Tribulation will also be martyred. There is really only one possible answer to counter this persuasive argument.

God does not intend his Church to experience his wrath. We have already seen that the Tribulation will be one of only two occasions when God vents his wrath on the whole of humanity. This will encompass the wrath of Satan (manifested through the Antichrist), but Revelation makes it very clear that God is orchestrating the pouring out of his own wrath (*Revelation 6:16-17; 15:1; 15:7*). While Christians may experience the malevolence of Satan, they are not destined for the wrath of God, as we saw in an earlier part of the chapter. The consequences of God's wrath would be that many believers would die alongside unbelievers in the unprecedented destruction of this time. Whereas resisting Satan's fury counts as endurance for Christians, it is hard to see that death through the wars and destruction of this time would in anyway be meaningful or refining.

2. Many believers will be martyred during the Tribulation

There are several passages in the mid-section of Revelation which refer to the martyrdom of the saints. Some would seem to be references to historical martyrdom (*Revelation 6:9-11* and *16:4-6*), but *Revelation 7:9-17* and *Revelation 20:4* imply that a great many will have been martyred during the Tribulation. Large numbers of martyred saints during the Tribulation is a challenge to the pre-tribulation rapture, because it means they must all have come from Tribulation converts. Will so many have been converted during this time? We do not know, but it is a legitimate objection.

3. Revelation hints at extensive evangelism during the Tribulation

Many Christians believe there will be extensive evangelism during the Tribulation and that this will be accompanied by the persecution and martyrdom of many Christians. The question arises as to who does the evangelizing if the Church has been removed beforehand. This is not an insurmountable problem. *Revelation Chapter 7* talks of 144,000 Jewish men being sealed by God and these may be used to bring many

Jews and Gentiles to faith during this time. It is also possible that the sudden removal of the Church of true believers is likely to make many people, perhaps with a nominal attachment to Christianity, wonder what has happened, and to decide to put their faith in God. It also seems likely that as the Tribulation worsens many people will cry out to God for mercy. (It should however be noted, that Revelation itself says that despite the worsening situation, many will not call for mercy, but will curse God instead! *Revelation 16:9, 11* and *21.*)

4. Why did the apostle Paul need to explain the Man of Lawlessness to the Thessalonians?

John Piper raises a significant point in favour of the post-tribulation view.[6] In *2 Thessalonians Chapter 2* the apostle Paul is attempting to put at rest the minds of the believers who seem to have been told (wrongly) that *the day of the Lord* had already happened. Paul reassures them that *the day of the Lord* will not come unless the rebellion[7] comes first and the man of lawlessness (the Antichrist) is revealed. Piper's point is that if the Church is caught away in a pre-tribulation rapture then they will neither see the seven year tribulation nor the Antichrist, so why would Paul give them this indicator unless they themselves would experience these events? Put another way why did he not say: "You know *the day of the Lord* has not come, because the Rapture has not happened and you are still here"?

It is still possible that Paul is referring to the Rapture in *2 Thessalonians 2:1* when he refers to *"the coming of our Lord Jesus Christ and our being gathered to him,"* and to the Tribulation and the Second Advent of the Lord from verse 2 onwards. However, John Piper does have a point that we should take seriously.

Here are two further, but less powerful arguments for a post-tribulation rapture:

5. Matthew 24:29-31 indicates a post-tribulation Rapture

This passage of scripture is often considered to be a strong argument in favour of this position:

> *Immediately after the tribulation of those days the sun will be darkened... Then will appear in heaven the sign of the Son of*

Man, and then all the tribes of the earth will mourn, and they will see the Son of Man coming on the clouds of heaven with power and great glory. And he will send out his angels with a loud trumpet call, and they will gather his elect from the four winds, from one end of heaven to the other.

(Matthew 24:29-31)

If the elect refers to the Church then they will be gathered after the Tribulation. The trumpet call would then coincide with the trumpet in *1 Thessalonians 4:16*. However, there are two reservations concerning this view. Some writers believe the word 'gather' is more likely to refer to gathering the elect of Israel who still remain worldwide, and restoring them to the land of Israel. Ezekiel says, *"I will leave none of them remaining among the nations any more."* (*Ezekiel 39:28*). This prophecy would then apply to Jews still in the worldwide Diaspora, who are gathered to Israel at that time. A further, perhaps more convincing point, is that the text refers to the gathering from heaven rather than the earth and thus it could refer to the gathering of the saints already in heaven to accompany Christ on his return to earth. The location and the meaning of the word 'elect' in this passage cannot be discerned conclusively.

6. The pre-tribulation Rapture is a recent eschatology

The pre-tribulation rapture has appeared relatively recently on the theological scene and so it carries less weight than other eschatological views. It only came into existence in the early 1800s through the dispensational teaching of J N Darby and has caught on in the last two centuries. According to this view such teaching was not present in the early Church. It is true that the early Church Fathers were unanimous in their view that the Rapture would be post-tribulational.[8]

This argument presumes that all doctrine was understood by the early Church, whereas a case can also be made that God reveals the meaning of Scripture as history unfolds. We have only to think how the Holy Spirit has restored doctrines that had largely been lost to the Church, to understand that biblical doctrine has not been a fixture in the Church: justification by faith, full immersion baptism and the gifts of the Holy Spirit are some of the major doctrines to have been restored in the last 500 years.

However, there is a further weakness in this argument. It hinges on the attitude of the early Church to the majority of Jews who did not accept the Christian message that Jesus Christ was in fact their Messiah. This led to a rift between the two communities which in turn led to the teaching of replacement theology[9] which held that the Church had taken the place of Israel as the people of God. The early Church did not expect the Jews to be restored to their ancient land. That meant, by default, that it must be the Church which goes through the Tribulation. For this reason they could not envisage a rapture prior to the Tribulation. This view persisted among premillennialists for the next 1700 years. Whether the Rapture is pre- or post-tribulational, this argument demonstrates that we need to be very clear about the significance of the Jews and Israel in these end-times. **They are significant.**

The Mid-tribulation and Pre-wrath raptures

This is an appropriate point at which to consider these minority positions.[10] Both the mid-tribulation rapture and the pre-wrath rapture argue that the Church experiences the persecution of man in the form of the Antichrist, but avoids the wrath of God which is manifested in the second half of the Tribulation (the Great Tribulation). In this way they are able to affirm the scriptures which say that we are not destined to receive the wrath of God. These views also have the merit that they would answer John Piper's argument in Section 4: by the mid-point of the Tribulation the Church would have knowledge of the Antichrist and his purposes and so Paul would have had reason to alert the believers.

The mid-tribulation view argues that the wrath of God begins when the Antichrist turns against the Jews and sets himself up in the Temple, while the pre-wrath position moves the rapture closer to the return of Christ to earth. It argues that *the day of the Lord* (the time of God's wrath) is preceded by the celestial signs that include the darkening of the sun and the blood red colour of the Moon and that these herald the return of Christ. This makes the duration of the wrath of God even shorter.

The problem for me with both these views is that they restrict the wrath of God entirely to the second half of the Tribulation. A reading of Revelation does not warrant the distinction between the Antichrist's wrath against the Jews and the Saints on the one hand and God's wrath against sinful humanity on the other. God's wrath and the activities of the Antichrist seem to unfold simultaneously. The whole of the tribulation is clearly a bad time on earth. It has been suggested that the wrath of God commences with the sixth or seventh seal. However, I think there is no reason to believe that the wrath of God does not begin with the opening of the seven seals and the four *Horsemen of the Apocalypse,* or that this does not happen in the first half of the Tribulation. Once again we are talking about possibilities, rather than probabilities or certainties.

Conclusion

By this time readers will probably have been overwhelmed by the different views and the various arguments! Hopefully they will have realised that it is not a straightforward matter to arrive at a pre- or post-tribulation position on the Rapture. There are significant reasons for holding one or the other view (or even one of the minority views).

Nevertheless, I still think the balance of evidence favours a pre-tribulation rapture. For me the three most powerful arguments are:

1. *Matthew Chapter 24* seems to describe two very different aspects to Jesus' return – one very visible and one in stealth. I do not see how these can be combined in a single event.

2. The scriptures indicate that we are not destined to receive the wrath of God. I do not see how we can avoid this wrath if we have to go through the Tribulation.

3. Why would Jesus warn us to be prepared for his unexpected return, if it were not possible to avoid the Tribulation? The warning would have little meaning once we are in the Tribulation and can expect his return at the end of it.

However, we cannot be certain. We cannot find a knockout argument for one view or the other. Perhaps God has set it up this way. Throughout the Bible we see that he always wants us to live by faith in him. Perhaps he wants us to be prepared for either eventuality. He wants us to be prepared and faithfully going about the work he has set for us should Jesus return secretly to rapture his Church. Equally he wants us to prepare to endure the Tribulation should we have to go through it. If we knew for certain that he would rapture the Church in advance of the Tribulation it would be very easy to relax and wait for it to happen. If we knew for certain that we would go through the Tribulation, then we could fall into inactivity through depression. This way we stay alert and ready, as Jesus commanded.

I still hope the Church will be raptured before the Tribulation, but I cannot be as certain as I used to be.

NOTES

1. Various suggestions have been made as to how this will happen. One is that Christ will be airborne and will circle the earth sufficient times for "every eye to see him". A more mundane view is that television will enable everyone to see his arrival in the air and in Jerusalem.

2. See the alternative view on the meaning of these verses in Chapter 5, Note 1.

3. Some writers argue that the virgins represent two sets of Christians, those who are ready and those who are not, and that the latter get excluded from the marriage to Christ, the Bridegroom. However, in the traditional Jewish wedding the virgins are not the bride, but companions to the bride, and so this seems more likely to be a simple story about the need to be ready.

4. Several passages of scripture indicate that Christ will return accompanied by saints and angels. (See *1 Thessalonians 3:13; Jude 14-15; Mathew 24:29-31; 2 Thessalonians 1:7*)

5. The Greek word translated *begging* suggests a strong form of prayer, such as 'entreating' or 'beseeching'. All translations use the verb 'to escape'. The King James Version says:

    Watch ye therefore, and pray always, that you may be accounted worthy to escape all these things that shall come to pass, and to stand before the Son of Man.

6. See John Piper's article on the Internet, <http://www.desiringgod.org/sermons/what-must-happen-before-the-day-of-the-lord>

7. Rebellion in this context is defined as apostasy or falling away from the faith.

8. There was one writer Pseudo-Ephraem, the Syrian, who appears to have argued for a pre-tribulation rapture. This is disputed by the other side, but either way I think it is unwise to attach too much importance to one writer, particularly as there is uncertainty as to the date of his document which could have been written anytime between AD 374 and 627.

9. See my book, *Has God really finished with Israel?* Chapter 10.

10. An account of the mid-tribulation rapture can be found in *Three Views on the Rapture Pre-, Mid-, or Post-tribulation* (see Section 3 by Gleason L. Archer), while an account of the pre-wrath rapture can be found in *Antichrist before the day of the Lord* by Alan Kurschner.

7 THE BIBLE – HOW TO APPROACH AND UNDERSTAND IT

The Church has always had a problem with how to address some of the themes of the Bible. The Church Fathers early on decided that the Old Testament passages referring to the restoration of the Jews to their ancient land were not to be taken literally, but were to be seen as symbolic of the new creation, the Church, which had taken Israel's place. This was the theme of my book: *Has God really finished with Israel?* in which I devoted a chapter to the importance of understanding the Old Testament in as literal a way as possible.

The Catholic, and later the Orthodox Churches, began to change the emphasis or meaning of New Testament doctrines relating to Jesus and salvation. In the Catholic Church emphasis was put on the need to earn one's salvation through good works as well as faith and believers were directed to the supposed mediatorial qualities of Mary, the mother of Jesus. Until the Middle Ages ordinary people were not able to read the scriptures for themselves (either because they were illiterate or because the scriptures were in Latin) and were thus at the Church's mercy in terms of what they learnt and were encouraged to believe. It was only when the scriptures were translated into their native tongue that they could find out what the scriptures actually said. In England this was due to the pioneering work of men like John Wycliffe and William Tyndale. It met with strident opposition from the Catholic Church and William Tyndale paid for it with his life, but it helped to return people to the truth of the scriptures during the Reformation.

The subject of the end-times and the return of Jesus has also been a subject of controversy and debate as we have already seen with the various approaches to the Millennium taken in history. This is understandable given the fact that the principal book in the Bible about the end-times, the book of Revelation, is written in very symbolic terms. Other apocalyptic literature, such as Daniel, is also written using symbolism and allegory. However, as we have already seen, this symbolism does actually represent events and by matching scripture with scripture it is possible to ascertain what much of it means. We need to remember too that the Bible has been written for ordinary people and it should not be too arduous for them to discern its meaning.[1] It is true that God has ordained teachers of Scripture. We see this in the New Testament as one of the offices in the Church along with apostles, prophets, evangelists and pastors (*1 Corinthians 12:28; Ephesians 4:11*). Nevertheless, as Scripture itself states this does not give them liberty to depart from the meaning of Scripture. The apostle James states that biblical teachers will be judged more strictly than others (*James 3:1*).

Such departure has been a problem throughout the Church age, and despite the Reformation, it reached new heights with 'higher criticism' studies of the Bible in the late nineteenth and early twentieth centuries. Essential biblical doctrines such as Jesus' virgin birth, his atoning death on the Cross, and his resurrection have all been questioned and given alternative explanations. However, God has not been passive in the face of this biblical apostasy. The twentieth century has also seen the advent of the Pentecostal and Charismatic movements which has inspired the Church to go back to its roots in the Acts of the Apostles. The Church, or those willing within the Church, have been taken back to the way the early Church operated under the guidance of the Holy Spirit.

Before we go further into this subject this would be a good point at which to ask: what is the Bible, who wrote it and what purpose does it serve?

What is the Bible?

The Bible is God's Word to the human race. He has chosen to express himself through the writings of many different people. In the prophets we read the actual words that God spoke to their Jewish audiences, written down for posterity. In other writings the words are human thoughts or records of historical events. Many, perhaps most Christians, however, believe that these words have been inspired by the Holy Spirit, not least because the Bible says that about itself (see *2 Timothy 3:16* and *2 Peter 1:20-21*). It is a book about salvation and about the way we should live. It is a history book and a book about the future. It is a book of prose, but one which contains some beautiful poetry. This means that some of it is a straightforward account of both historical and future events, while other parts use literary devices such as simile, metaphor, allegory and apocalyptic symbol. Jesus himself used a special teaching device, the parable, which while not unique to the Bible, finds its most extensive use there. Parables had become an established method of teaching in the Middle East in Old Testament times.

Those who recognise this description of the Bible will also recognise that the Old and New Testaments are intimately linked, one leading into the other. We can say that the Old Testament and the New Testament form a coherent, seamless whole. The thread of salvation runs right through the Bible from *Chapter 3 of Genesis* to the end of *Revelation*.

A word of caution

For the most part the Bible can be read as a literal narrative of God's dealings with humanity. There may be issues around the dates of historical events and there are certainly gaps in the genealogies. There may be some minor contradictions in both dates and numbers, but not things which upset the literal understanding of what is being described. To give examples, the Bible's genealogies make fascinating reading, but we cannot make a complete genealogy from Adam and Eve through to Jesus Christ – the generations are said to be 'telescoped'.[2] We may read really meaningful books such as Job, but not be able to date its time in Old Testament history. One of the last kings of Judah, Jehoiachin, was described as eighteen years of age when he came to the throne in *2 Kings 24:8*, but only eight years in *2 Chronicles 36:9*, almost certainly a copying error in most Hebrew manuscripts; (the context shows that he must have been eighteen). However, these are not serious obstacles to a literal understanding of the narrative.

Nevertheless, when it comes to prophecy we do have to exercise caution, for two reasons. First of all, the prophecy does not usually have adequate information to pinpoint its future happening. However, when it has happened, it is then much easier to discern. Secondly, the language is sometimes metaphorical or allegorical. Symbolism is used instead of straight narrative. Let us examine these two points in more detail.

There are very few prophecies which are crystal clear about their future unfolding. The best example is the prophecy in Jeremiah about the return of the Jewish exiles from Babylon:

> *For thus says the Lord: When seventy years are completed for Babylon, I will visit you, and I will fulfil to you my promise and bring you back to this place.*
>
> (Jeremiah 29:10)

This is a clear Old Testament promise which happened as foretold. On the other hand the prophecies foretelling the birth of the future Messiah were also stated clearly, but there was little indication of the date of his arrival. These are the famous prophecies from Isaiah (*Isaiah 7:14; 9:6-7; 11:1-2*) about the birth of a child with some very special characteristics. No one anticipated the birth of Jesus, but the prophecies became clear after the event, as we know from the gospel writers.[3] Most Christians have no difficulty in accepting that these examples were prophecies and that they happened. Non-believers try to disparage such prophecies, but Christians believe that they have been fulfilled.

Metaphors and allegories

Coming to the second point, there are however prophecies which are presented as metaphors or allegories. In some instances the metaphor is immediately explained in the text. The best example of this is the well-known story of the Valley of Dry Bones in *Ezekiel Chapter 37*. Here God uses a vivid metaphor and then tells us that *"These bones are* (in other words *represent) the whole house of Israel"* (verse 11). The rest of the chapter then spells out very clearly, using another metaphor of the two sticks, how God will re-unite the house of Ephraim (Israel) with the house of Judah. The metaphors are vivid and the meaning quite clear. Those who would argue that the Israel referred to here (and in many other Old Testament prophecies) is a metaphor for the Church in the New Testament, have a problem to explain. Why would God use one set of metaphors whose meaning is so clearly defined and yet leave the reader to surmise that the **explanation** is a further metaphor?

In the book of Daniel the visions given to the prophet are much more like allegories. For me an allegory is an extended metaphor or one metaphor built upon another. God introduces Daniel to four great empires in a series of visions involving 'fearsome beasts'. We are told that these beasts represent the Babylonian, the Medo-Persian and the Greek empires and that there is one to follow, more terrible than the others, which is clearly the Roman Empire. However, these visions are interspersed with references to the distant future and Daniel is told in both *Chapters 8* and *12* to seal up the visions until the end-times. Unlike the Valley of the Dry Bones God deliberately held back the explanations of some of Daniel's visions.

Where allegories, such as those of Daniel, convey the future unfolding of awesome and troubling events they are known as **apocalyptic literature**, and their metaphors as apocalyptic symbols. The most symbolic of the Bible's books is of course Revelation. From *Chapter 4* until the end, Revelation is one long apocalyptic story. However, there are still passages which speak very literally – for example the one thousand year time-span usually known as the Millennium. However, we still have to be cautious, because the literal is mixed in with the allegorical imagery. We can surmise things, but not be dogmatic about them.

A common sense approach

So what do I mean when I say that I read the Bible literally? I start with Derek Prince's maxim:

God means what he says, and says what he means.

If one thinks of the character of God, it could hardly be otherwise. He certainly has secrets (see *Deuteronomy 29:29*) and he sometimes veils his meaning through metaphor and allegory until he is ready to unfold it, but he does not mislead us. My guiding principle is to try to understand the scriptures literally unless it is really not possible to do so. Even where the scriptures are written as symbolic imagery, I believe it is still right to recognise that this imagery does actually represent events.

I like the approach of the Messianic Christian leader Dan Juster who says that he understands the Bible in a **straightforward** way. This gets round the problem of taking every word or phrase in a literal way. The prophets frequently use poetic language:

> The wilderness and the dry land shall be glad; the desert shall rejoice and blossom like the crocus...
>
> (Isaiah 35:1)

No one believes that the desert and the wilderness will behave like people, but we have no difficulty in understanding that the natural environment will respond to how it is treated. God is said to roar like a lion (*Hosea 11:10*) and Jesus is described as the *"Lion of the tribe of Judah"* (*Revelation 5:5*). The simile and metaphor respectively convey a sense of power. However, earlier in the same chapter in Hosea, we find:

> ... but Assyria shall be their king, because they have refused to return to me.
>
> (Hosea 11:5)

There is no metaphor here: this is a literal prophecy and it was fulfilled when the northern kingdom of Israel went into captivity.

Our view of the Old Testament

Many modern theologians believe that we should view it through the lens of the New Testament. Lenses, of course, change the appearance of things and this is what happens when we adopt this approach. It is sometimes stated that the apostles' doctrine overrules that which has gone before, though it is not always clear what this is meant to mean.

My own view is that unless the teachings of Jesus and the apostles clearly indicate that something in the New Testament has replaced or superseded that which has existed in the Old Testament, then we should continue to treat the Old Testament as having application. The only clear-cut case where the New Testament does supersede the Old concerns the replacement of the Mosaic Covenant by the New Covenant, made applicable by the death and resurrection of Jesus. The writer of Hebrews (*Chapters 8* and *10*) clearly indicates that this replacement applies to the ceremonial law and the sacrificing of animals. It does not of course revoke the Ten Commandments which were the moral foundation of the Mosaic Law. In fact Jesus emphasised these commandments and made them even more demanding in the Sermon on the Mount (*Matthew Chapter 5*).

Consequently, we should be very careful not to downgrade the Old Testament. It is sometimes said that the writings of the apostle Paul have overridden the promises of the Abrahamic Covenant to the Jews. This is **not** true (see Appendix 2), nor is it true that the New Testament's apparent lack of reference to Israel and the restoration of the Jews to their ancient land transforms the promises made to them in the Old Testament.[4]

Summing up my approach (and that of many other Bible students) to a literal reading of the Bible, it means that I do not seek to superimpose an interpretation on the scriptures, especially those of the Old Testament. I take the passages as they come, reading them literally where possible. I suspend judgement on a definitive meaning to prophecies that are written as metaphor or allegory, unless the text explains the symbolism. It is also a wise approach because it honours what scripture itself says about prophecy:

> ... *that no prophecy of scripture is a matter of one's own interpretation, because no prophecy ever came by the impulse of man, but men moved by the Holy Spirit spoke from God.*
>
> (2 *Peter 1:20-21 RSV*)

Rules of Interpretation

Having made a plea for reading and understanding the Bible in a straightforward way are there any rules we should apply when studying Scripture?

The answer is yes, there are a few rules that help us to understand the Bible without upsetting the 'straightforward' approach to Scripture just described. Dr David Cooper (1886 – 1965) was a much respected scholar who founded the Bible Research Institute and he came up with a number of rules for interpreting the scriptures, of which four are helpful to our study of the end-times.

1. His first or **Golden Rule** encapsulated the views I have just expressed. It states in summary that:

   Biblical passages should be understood exactly as they are read unless there is an indication in the text that they should mean something else.[5]

   An extension of this rule is that a verse or a passage of scripture should not be taken out of the context in which it is written.

The following rules can then be applied within this overarching rule.

2. The **Rule of First Mention** states that:

   This requires one to go to the portion of scripture where a doctrine is first mentioned and study further examples of this doctrine in connection with the initial one. In this way the doctrine is built upon its foundation.

3. The **Rule of Double Reference** holds that:

   A passage of scripture may be speaking of two persons or events which are separated by a long interval of time, but which seem to be fused into one picture. This rule is particularly important for a correct understanding of prophecy.

4. The **Rule of Recurrence** states that:
    Some passages of scripture record an event which is then
    followed by a further passage on the same event which adds
    more detail to the first. It substantiates it.

I would add three of my own rules! These are particularly apt in the
study of the end-times.

5. *We should pay particular attention to the similarities between*
    passages which may not seem at first sight be discussing the same
    event. This is particularly helpful when comparing passages from the
    Old with the New Testament.
6. *Where we are unsure of the meaning of a particular passage then we*
    should say so! Let us state that it is supposition and perhaps present
    alternative views.
7. *If a theology or view of Scripture needs to leave out or minimize*
    important scriptures, then it is suspect.

Let us see how these rules work out in practice in relation to the
end-times.

The Golden Rule

An obvious application of Dr Cooper's golden rule is in relation to the
numerous Old Testament prophecies predicting the return of the Jews
to the land of Israel. I spent a major part of my book, *Has God really*
finished with Israel? arguing that these prophecies should be taken
literally. Many theologians want to transform them into metaphors or
allegories for the Church. The futility of this approach is seen in relation
to the metaphor of the Valley of Dry Bones (*Ezekiel Chapter 37*), which
I mentioned earlier in the chapter.

The Rule of First Mention

To examine this rule let us look at the person of the Antichrist.
This man is described in several chapters of the book of Daniel
(*Daniel 7:24-25; 8:23-26; 9:26-27* and *11:36-45*). He is called a
horn, a king and more specifically a man of bold countenance.
(These passages need to be read carefully, because in *Daniel*

Chapter 11 we have an example of 'double reference'.) This first appearance in Daniel sets the scene for what we learn about the Antichrist in the New Testament in *2 Thessalonians, 1 & 2 John* and *Revelation* where he is variously described as the man of lawlessness, the Antichrist and the beast. The reference in *1 John* opens up the possibility that there is a spirit of antichrist as well as a person. For us not to start with Daniel, would miss out important defining features of the Antichrist and the context in which he will operate.

The Rule of Double Reference

We can also apply this rule to Daniel's writing. In *Chapter 11* Daniel is given much detail about two of the four kingdoms and their kings which will arise following the death of Alexander the Great, the charismatic leader of the Greek empire. These are the king of the North (the Seleucid kingdom based in Syria) and the king of the South (the Ptolemaic kingdom in Egypt). From *verse 29* to *35* it would seem from the context that Daniel is describing one of the Seleucid kings, Antiochus IV Epiphanes, an evil king who desecrated the Jewish Temple in AD 167. However, from *verse 36* he clearly moves to describing a different, much later king whom we can discern as the Antichrist.

Another well-known example of double reference is found in *Isaiah Chapter 14* where for some of the time Isaiah is describing an earthly king of Babylon, but from *verse 12* to *14* he is clearly talking about a heavenly being who is generally recognised as Lucifer, the devil.

Because of the importance of this rule in prophecy I have given a full explanation of how it works in Appendix 3.

The Rule of Recurrence

An example of this rule related to the end-times is the war of Gog and Magog. Ezekiel in *Chapter 38* introduces us to this war while in *Chapter 39* he adds more detail. Interestingly, despite the amazing detail given by Ezekiel, it is difficult to place the time of this war in relation to the Tribulation, as I explain in Chapter 11, *What does the future hold?*

Another well-known example of the rule of recurrence is *Genesis Chapters 1* and *2*. Much more detail is given about the creation of man and woman in this second chapter.

Turning now to my own rules:

Watching for Similarities

A good example of this is found in relation to the *day of the Lord* and the Tribulation. The two are synonymous, but this may not seem so at first sight. However, when we compare the signs of God's wrath concerning the *day of the Lord* in the Old Testament (for example, *Isaiah 13:6-13; Joel 2:30-31* and *Zephaniah 1:14-18*), with the descriptions in Jesus' Olivet discourse (*Matthew Chapter 24*) and the judgements of God in Revelation, we see they are describing one and the same event.

Confessing Uncertainty

It is wise to confess our uncertainties about the precise meaning of certain unfulfilled prophecies. Attention to this practice by writers on the end-times would have held back the suspicion of many Christians that some writers are simply guessing the future. Making predictions which do not materialize discredits biblical prophecy at a time when we ought to be taking it very seriously. It is the unshakeable conviction with which some writers express their views about the unfolding of future prophecy which is even more damaging than an occasional error.

Ignoring or minimizing important scriptures

This is perhaps the most important error. As we have seen there are a number of views of the end-times, based on Christians' views of the Millennium. However, some of these views involve ignoring distinct passages of Scripture. The Antichrist is a case in point. An end-time theology which ignores a personified Antichrist and says that it represents evil, or a particular time of evil, is ignoring what Scripture actually says. As we have seen there is enough evidence to identify a major figure in history who has come to be known as the Antichrist. For me this must be built into a biblical view of the end-times. If it is not, then the millennial view will be in error.

Conclusion

I hope the reader will have been persuaded both from my opening chapter and from this one of the value of understanding Scripture in a straightforward way. I acknowledge the benefit of having some rules to help us understand Scripture, though I am reluctant to call them 'laws' as one will find in some theological writings. A search of the literature on the Internet will show that Bible teachers down the ages have come up with many rules or guidelines. I would argue that we should keep these to a minimum. Textual and linguistic analysis of the original Hebrew or Greek script is important and I am prepared to trust the scholars who have made the authoritative translations of the Bible that we now use. I myself look to various versions of the Bible for different angles on a particular verse, but where a doctrine of Scripture is said to hinge on the meaning of particular words then I am very wary. As I mentioned earlier I believe the Bible has been written for ordinary people and I am happy to trust that God has made his message clear, through the authoritative translations he has ordained to be written.

NOTES

1. *Psalm 119:130* expresses the view that the Bible is written for ordinary people. (The word *simple* is not used in a negative sense here; it means *ordinary*.)

2. See Dr John Millam for a very full discussion of this subject in the Genesis Genealogies: Are they complete?

   <http://www.godandscience.org/youngearth/genesis_genealogies.html>

3. Simeon and the prophetess Anna, both mentioned in *Luke Chapter 2*, seemed to have foreknowledge of the birth of Christ, but that was very close to the event.

   It can be argued that *Numbers 24:17* provided a clue to the time of the Messiah's arrival in the prophecy of Balaam: *"A star shall come out of Jacob (Israel)...".* Clearly the wise men (astronomers) who came looking for the King of the Jews (*Matthew 2:1-2*) were anticipating a star that would indicate the arrival of this king. However, the Jewish leaders showed no indication of this knowledge, though they did know the place of his birth (*verse 4-5*).

4.   I deal with this subject very fully in my book, *Has God really finished with Israel?*

5.   Dr David Cooper's Golden Rule in full:

> *When the plain sense of scripture makes common sense, seek no other sense; therefore, take every word at its primary, ordinary, usual, literal meaning unless the facts of the immediate context, studied in the light of related passages and axiomatic and fundamental truths indicate clearly otherwise.*

For his full rules of interpretation go to:

<http://www.biblicalresearch.info/page7.html>

8 *A CRITIQUE OF THE DIFFERENT MILLENNIAL VIEWS*

A literal or symbolic approach

The fundamental issue we need to distinguish is whether the viewpoint takes a symbolic or a literal approach to the scriptures concerning the end-times. It is recognised by both approaches that the apocalyptic books such as Daniel, the Olivet discourse in both Matthew and Luke, and Revelation itself use much symbolism and many metaphors. However, that does not mean that we can be liberal in our interpretation of this symbolism. The descriptions in both Daniel and Revelation are extremely detailed, a fact which suggests they have specific meanings. It is also significant, as we have seen earlier, that there are striking similarities between accounts in the different apocalyptic books. We have seen how the darkening of the sun, moon and stars is referred to in *Isaiah 13:6-13, Joel 2:31* and *Revelation 8:12*. Furthermore we meet an individual man in *Daniel, 2 Thessalonians* and *Revelation* who personifies evil. His name is different in each case, but the context demonstrates that the writers are describing the same man, a man we now call the Antichrist. To suppose that the Antichrist is a system of evil rather than a significant individual is to deny the validity of these three descriptions.

The **literal approach** says that we should take a passage as having a literal meaning unless it is really impossible to do this. This means, for example, that the seventieth week of Daniel which describes the time of the '*king of bold countenance*' (*Daniel 8:23*) is a specific period of seven years.[1] If we say that the Tribulation spans the whole period between the First and Second Advents of Christ we are not anchoring this to any scripture. Likewise if we say that the apocalyptic events of Daniel, the Olivet discourse and Revelation all took place in the period around AD 70 with the destruction of the Temple, we cannot explain many specific prophecies such as the covenant made between the 'king of bold countenance' and the Jews. Most important of all, however, this reasoning completely detaches the return of Jesus from all these events, which are described in the apocalyptic passages as happening shortly before his return.[2]

The apocalyptic passages of Daniel, the Olivet discourse and Revelation clearly indicate that Christ's arrival on earth closes this time of trouble (see *Daniel 2:31-35 & 44-45; Matthew 24:29-31* and *Revelation 19:11-21*). The literal approach also requires us to recognise that Christ returns to a world manifestly in need of his help. Human society will have become morally bankrupt and evil and be in need of radical surgery.

The one thousand-year Millennium

Some theologians are unhappy with the idea of a literal 1000-year Millennium, principally on the grounds that this figure is not repeated elsewhere in the Bible. However, it is a specific time period and in the absence of contradictory evidence, there is no reason not to take it as such. The thousand years is mentioned six times in the relevant passage (*Revelation 20:1-10*).

Even though they appear close together in Revelation it is a mistake to coalesce the Millennium with the new heaven and earth (*Revelation Chapters 21* and *22*). There are several reasons for this. The first is that the new heaven and earth, mentioned in *Revelation Chapter 21* are clearly differentiated from what has happened during the Millennium (*Revelation Chapter 20*). Evil is still found during this time and Satan is not finally dealt with until the end of the thousand years when he is thrown into hell (the lake of fire and sulphur). This is followed by the Great White Throne judgement which determines or confirms people's eternal destinies. Only with the new heaven and earth do we finally meet a universe where evil has been banished.

The second reason is that there are passages in Isaiah which appear to speak about the Millennium and describe things which will certainly not happen in eternity when all things are made new. Thus in *Isaiah 11:1-9* and *Isaiah 65:20* we find a time of peace and quiet ruled over by the Lord who at the same time is said to judge the world with equity and severity. Wickedness is still said to exist among mortal men and women and although they will live to a ripe old age, the sinner is said to die accursed in his sin. We know this cannot apply to the new heaven and earth described in *Revelation Chapter 21* since by then sin will have been banished and death will be a thing of the past, "*the former things have passed away*" (*Revelation 21:4*). It is thus very clear that the Millennial reign of Christ is very different from the new heaven and earth. Furthermore, the Lord is very much in charge in the Millennium:

> They [the saints] came to life and reigned with Christ for a
> thousand years.
>
> *(Revelation 20:4)* [comment added]

By contrast in the new heaven and earth, in other words in eternity, Christ will have handed back his authority to the Father (*1 Corinthians 15:24-28*).

It is through this kind of reasoning that we can unpack the truths surrounding the end-times. This does not mean that we can be certain about every event described which is why I have avoided a detailed analysis of Revelation. However, we can make an analysis which gives an accurate overall picture of the end-times.

The significance of Israel and the Jewish people

The other issue we need to address in assessing the validity of the different Millennial positions is the importance they attach to the Jews and Israel in God's purposes for the end-times. I spent some time in Chapter 3 explaining why the central part of *Revelation Chapters* 4 to

18 is about Israel and not about the Church. I accept that we cannot rule out the Church being on earth at this time and we know too that many Jews and Gentiles will come to faith during this time and may well be martyred for their faith. However, we have examined in depth (Chapter 6) the arguments in favour of either a pre-tribulation or a post-tribulation rapture.

Whether the Church goes through some or all of the Tribulation or departs beforehand, the Tribulation period is pre-eminently about God's dealings with the Jews and his wrath expressed towards the Gentile nations who turn to the Antichrist rather than to God. I believe the evidence for this is conclusive.

Where does this leave the respective Millennial positions?

It would seem to rule out those positions which do one or more of the following things:

1. Treat events like the Tribulation and the Antichrist only in symbolic terms.
2. Minimise God's wrath and the significance of the day of the Lord.
3. Do not separate the Millennium from the new heaven and earth.
4. See Christ as returning to a world so improved by Christian morality and government that it is ready to receive a reigning King.
5. Either discount or minimise the role of the Jews and Israel in the period just prior to Christ's return.

If these five viewpoints are correct this would rule out the amillennial and the postmillennial positions and their variants.

Amillennialism
Amillennialism has the merit that it emphasises Christ's rule in our hearts and that through the Church age this has been a significant aspect of the kingdom of God. Its approach highlights the words of Jesus to Pontius Pilate:

My kingdom is not of this world. If my kingdom were of this world, my servants would have been fighting, that I might not be delivered over to the Jews.

(John 18:36)

However, there is a tension in the scriptures between the next world and this world. It is true that the change of heart in a new believer is what matters for eternity and that this change can impact the present world, but only up to a point. The large majority of people are not believers, Satan still roams this earth (*1 Peter 5:8*), false religions abound and the world has in recent times become a morally worse and dangerous place. It demands a resolution which the return of Christ brings in a very tangible way.

Christ's words to Pilate did not rule out a restoration of the earthly kingdom to the Jews. This was still very much on the minds of the apostles just prior to Jesus' ascension to heaven when they asked him:

Lord, will you at this time restore the kingdom to Israel?

(Acts 1:6)

He responded by saying:

It is not for you to know times or seasons that the Father has fixed by his own authority.

(Acts 1:7)

The implication of this is a positive one: *"yes, the kingdom will be restored, but it is not the time for you to know when."* The reason for this was that Jesus had work for them to do in the intervening period:

But you will receive power when the Holy Spirit has come upon you, and you will be my witnesses in Jerusalem and in all Judea and Samaria, and to the end of the earth.

(Acts 1:8)

If there was to be no kingdom restoration, then this was the time for Jesus to say: *"you have got it wrong; the kingdom of God is now in the hearts of men and women. There is no need for a restoration of the physical kingdom to Israel."* He did not say this. What he did was to indicate a delay. There was other work for his disciples to do.

We then find this earthly kingdom referred to again at the end of the New Testament. It is the Millennium of *Revelation Chapter 20* in which Jesus will reign as King from Jerusalem and Israel will play a leading role. Aspects of this kingdom are described in various Old Testament passages, as we shall see in Chapter 10. Should anyone doubt the reality of Israel's restoration as a kingdom, I would encourage him or her to read *Ezekiel 37:24-28* and *47:13* to *48:29* inclusive. Detailed instructions are given as to how the land should be divided among the twelve tribes of Israel.[3] It should be noted (*Ezekiel 47:22-23*) that the Israelites are to give an inheritance to non-Jews living among them as if they were native-born children of Israel. God will be fair to the Arabs and other ethnic groups.

By concentrating on the spiritual aspects of God's kingdom to the exclusion of an earthly kingdom, the amillennialists have relegated or ignored the many events described in the apocalyptic passages in both the Old and New Testaments. I have attempted to demonstrate that the Jews are central to the end-times, that the Tribulation is a very tangible event and that the Antichrist will be a very real person. One simply cannot dismiss these things as symbolically representative of historical events or impersonal evil. It is when we align the apocalyptic passages in the Old Testament with those in the New Testament that the events and people come sharply into focus.

Finally, a word on *Preterism:*[4] classical amillennialism holds that the events of the Tribulation have unfolded throughout history, while preterists believe that many, if not all of the apocalyptic events described in Jesus' Olivet discourse and the book of Revelation, happened at the time of the Jewish revolts between AD 66 and AD 135. In their view Revelation would be a symbolic outworking of the Olivet discourse. Now it is true that some of the Olivet discourse applies to the destruction of the Temple in AD 70, but not all of it. Much of the Olivet discourse clearly refers to the end-times (see Chapter 3). Furthermore, preterists would have difficulty in relating most of Revelation to the very specific events which occurred during Rome's destruction of Jerusalem and the Temple. Revelation is painted with a much broader brush and applies to the whole earth. It simply cannot be compressed into the events surrounding the destruction of the Temple and Jerusalem between AD 70 and AD 135.

Postmillennialism

Postmillennialism has one significant merit which unfortunately tends to obscure its weaknesses. Its great merit is that is seeks to see the world won for Christ. No evangelical Christian can afford to ignore the importance of this motivation; Christ commands us to evangelise the world (*Matthew 28:18-20; Mark 16:15-18; Luke 24:47-49* and *Acts 1:8*).

Starting in the nineteenth century with the great missionary movements, much of the world was evangelised by the end of the twentieth century. However, there are still many people groups who have not yet been reached, notably in South East Asia, and there is of course the huge Muslim population across North Africa and the Middle East which remained largely untouched by the earlier missionary movements.[5] (There is heartening evidence today that God is very much at work among Muslims in the Middle East.) Despite this expansion of Christianity in the twentieth century there has not been a reduction in evil and an extension of righteousness in world governments. The mistake has been to forget that Satan would step up his activity in the end-times as his demise approached. We do have the kingdom of God in the hearts of believers, but we do not see this reflected in righteous government. The situation has got worse: developed societies are moving away from Christian values. The scriptures warn us of a falling away from the Christian faith as the end-times approach (see *1 Timothy 4:1-3; 2 Timothy 3:1-5*). We have certainly seen this in much of Western society over the last half-century. It is this parallel growth of evil which undermines the postmillennial case.

Dominion Postmillennialism has taken the nineteenth century ambition of spreading the gospel across the whole world, one stage further. It claims that where the gospel has been taken, it is then possible to roll back the dominion of darkness (Satan's kingdom) and establish righteous government in the nations of the world. The difficulty with this theology is that it is deceptively attractive. Who among us does not want to see Satan's kingdom rolled up for good? It is clear, however, that the world at large is not becoming a better place. Satan's parallel activity (sovereignly permitted by God) is making the world spiritually darker. This is what the scriptures warn us to expect. It does not mean that local churches should not pray and work for social as well as spiritual improvement within their sphere of influence. However, we should not expect a righteous millennial reign by the Church prior to Christ's return, when the scriptures indicate that he will introduce such a reign following his physical return to earth.

Premillennialism

Having examined the weaknesses in the case for amillennialism and postmillennialism, we are left with premillennialism. This does seem to be the most viable overarching eschatology for the end-times. We have seen that there are two major strands to premillennialism, so that it cannot be a uniformly correct approach. However, it does meet most of the criteria mentioned earlier in the chapter.

1. It treats the Tribulation as a literal, climactic period at the close of the Church age prior to the return of Christ and it treats the Antichrist as a real individual, manifesting the works of Satan. It also sees the Tribulation as the outworking of God's wrath in *the day of the Lord*.

2. It treats the Millennium as a period of time (1000 years) distinct from the new heaven and new earth of eternity.

3. It sees Christ returning to a world where many souls have been won for him, but also one where spiritual darkness has increased.

4. While not all premillennialist are agreed on this, the viewpoint does provide the opportunity to treat Israel and the Jews as significant in the end-times prior to the return of Jesus.

It is for these reasons that I consider Premillennialism to be the correct view of the end-times, the Second Advent of Jesus Christ and the Millennium. While the timing of the Rapture is important to those who hold their respective views, we cannot make it a determinant of which premillennial view is correct. Premillennialists are not themselves agreed.

NOTES

1. See Appendix 1 on the measurement of time in the Bible.

2. In Daniel Jesus is not mentioned as such, but reference to a *"a stone was cut out by no human hand"* (*Daniel 2:34-35, 45*) and *"one like a son of man"* (*Daniel 7:13-14*) are clear references to the Lord.

3. It may well be possible to distinguish the tribes by DNA testing at this time. We can rest assured that God knows whom he deems to belong to a particular tribe.

4. I dealt with Preterism as an eschatology in Chapter 2. This included a substantial note (Note 5) on Partial and Full Preterism.

5. Helpful information on numbers of Christians, both general and evangelical, is given by organisations such as Pew Research. I also include The Lausanne Movement website with its article on how organisations such as *Operation World* and the *World Christian Database* arrive at numbers of evangelical Christians:

   <http://www.pewforum.org/2011/12/19/global-christianity-movements-and-denominations/>

   <http://conversation.lausanne.org/en/conversations/detail/11972#article_page_1>

   However, it should be understood that it is very difficult to assess the number of born-again believers. Surveys such as those mentioned above inevitably categorise Christians as evangelical, pentecostal and charismatic and so there is bound to be overlap among these categories which will tend to bring the actual number down. I have opted for a global figure of about 500 million in this book, **but I claim no particular validity for this figure.**

   Information about people groups still to be reached can be found on the Internet. A helpful map of unreached peoples is found at: <joshuaproject.net/global_statistics>

9 THE MYSTERY OF BABYLON

And on her forehead was written a name of mystery: "Babylon the great, mother of prostitutes and of earth's abominations."
(Revelation 17:5)

Babylon and its evils have been both a place and a theme right through the Bible from Nimrod and the tower of Babel in *Genesis Chapters 10 and 11*. It is necessary to address it in a study such as this because Revelation devotes two whole chapters to Babylon: its nature as a system of religion, its offence to God and its final destruction. To understand why it gets this attention in Revelation it is necessary to understand its offence to God. **It is an abomination in God's sight.** It is the mother of all pagan religions and represents a challenge to God and his plan of salvation through his Son Jesus Christ. As we shall see, it has succeeded in deceiving his chosen people, the Jews, and it has also found its way into the Christian Church. The pagan idolatry adopted by the Jews prior to their exile in the eighth and sixth centuries BC hugely damaged their relationship with God and opened the way to the curses spoken of by Moses in *Deuteronomy Chapter 28*. The Church, with its focus on salvation through Jesus, has avoided the wholesale embrace of pagan religion. Nevertheless, this religion has made many inroads into the Catholic and mainstream churches. Few Christians (including this author until a few years ago!) realise that Christmas and Easter are essentially pagan festivals with Christian events superimposed.[1] The Catholic adulation of Mary the mother of Jesus bears a striking resemblance to the worship of the Queen of heaven mentioned below.

Mystery: Babylon in the end-times

It seems that by the time we reach *Mystery: Babylon* in the book of Revelation it has become the dominant worldwide religion which has subsumed the world's other faiths. This is supposition, but there is strong evidence to support this view:

1. Even today, just as influential people in the secular world are discussing the need for world government, so religious leaders are talking of the need for the different faiths to cooperate and work together to sustain world peace.

2. As the Antichrist seeks to dominate the world politically and economically so he will want to dominate its religion (see *Revelation 13:5-10*). He will aspire to be worshipped himself, with the able assistance of the false prophet (*Revelation 13:11-18*). *Mystery: Babylon* may well be the worldwide religion which facilitates this worship. It appears that only the Christians will be in opposition to this universal worship of the Antichrist, and their lives will be in danger because of it.

3. *Revelation Chapter 17* reveals a close relationship between the Antichrist and the woman with the name *Mystery: Babylon the great, mother of prostitutes and of earth's abominations*. She is said both to be seated on many waters (many peoples and nations) and also on a scarlet beast who is clearly the Antichrist. Later the Antichrist turns against this woman or prostitute and destroys her. This speaks of a worldwide religion working in tandem with the Antichrist, but whose power later comes to threaten his.

While it is of course right to have good civil relationships with people of other faiths, attempts by Christian leaders to embrace or validate other faiths including pagan religion, cannot be pleasing to God. In the end-times we may find a worldwide, unified 'Church' with Christian beliefs in a melting pot with those of other faiths. As we explore this subject we shall see that God has been longsuffering, but in Revelation his patience with Babylon and its many tentacles comes to an abrupt end. *Mystery: Babylon* is one of the principal objects of God's wrath in the Tribulation.

Nimrod and the Tower of Babel

To have any hope of understanding *Mystery: Babylon* we have to go back to the rebellion against God in the time following Noah and the Flood. It seems to have been led by Noah's great-grandson Nimrod (*Genesis 10:8-12*). The name Nimrod is of Hebrew origin and biblical authorities generally agree that the word means rebel or rebellious. Little is said about him, but it is clear that he was a strong leader and warrior, a builder of cities and the first person to build an empire or kingdom. He brought the cities of Babel (Babylon), Erech, Accad and Calneh together in his kingdom in the land of Shinar (Mesopotamia). He later moved north to Assyria and built the great city of Nineveh. Although not stated as such, it seems likely that Nimrod would have been instrumental in building the Tower of Babel.

Babylon – city or religion?

Babylon was both a city in Mesopotamia (modern-day Iraq) and a place which gave rise to an idolatrous, pagan system of worship. The religious system of Babylon seems to have spawned many if not most idolatrous systems around the world. It is the parent of pagan worship and in particular that associated with the mother and child: goddess and son, the goddess being called the 'Queen of heaven'. Nimrod would have had direct knowledge of God and how to relate to him from his grandparents' generation (Ham, Japheth and Shem) and perhaps even from Noah himself. It is interesting to see how rebellion – shifting attention from God to oneself – leads to a false religion. We are wired for a relationship with God. Rebellion against this inevitably shifts attention to an alternative, idolatrous religion, a fact generally seized upon by Satan. *Genesis Chapter 11* makes clear that the building of the Tower of Babel was an act of defiance against God, serious enough for him to come down to earth and to confuse people's languages and thus lead to the dispersal of the human race across the earth.[2]

We shall later explore some of the many religions which originated with Babylon. Meanwhile, we need to recognise that Satan and his fallen angels (angelic princes and powers, see

Ephesians 6:12) are behind these false religions though men and women are often willing participants. One of the reasons why pagan religion, however well disguised, has had such a hold on the human race, is that whatever happens in history with the rise and fall of empires and their religious practices, the controlling satanic spirits behind them do not go away. They simply disguise the false religion or practice in a new form. The satanic Prince of Persia described in the book of Daniel (*Daniel 10:13*) is still likely to be operating in that part of the world. Several Christian writers have observed that the practice of placating the spirit of Molech, by sacrificing children to fire in ancient Canaan, finds a parallel in the modern-day sacrifice of children as suicide bombers in the Middle East.

So far we have discussed Babylon as a religious system, but it was also a significant city for many centuries. It was the capital city of kingdoms, and gave its name to the early and later Babylonian empires. It has been a ruin for many centuries now, although it continued to be a habitable city until the early centuries AD, but without the significance it had in the days of the Babylonian and Medo-Persian empires. It began to diminish in importance in the days of Alexander the Great from 323 BC. However, in the twentieth, and now in the twenty-first century, interest has been shown in excavating and restoring it. Photos on Google Earth show the ruins to be extensive and impressive, particularly where they have been restored. While not a realistic proposition at the present time, it is not impossible that it will be rebuilt as a modern city.

Christians are divided about this. Some think its present ruinous state fits the destruction described several times in Isaiah and Jeremiah and thus represents its final demise.[3] The problem with this view is that Babylon's gradual decline in history does not equate with the vivid climactic destruction described in *Revelation Chapter 18.* I shall return to this subject at the very end of the chapter. For the time being, I shall concentrate on Babylon as an idolatrous system. However, having argued that so much of Revelation should be taken literally and that the symbolism, where it occurs, clearly represents people and events, we should not rush to dismiss the possibility of the city of Babylon itself being rebuilt.

The myth behind Mystery: Babylon

So far I have avoided dealing with the myths that surround *Mystery: Babylon*, but it is necessary to examine one in particular because it does serve to explain the nature of this idolatrous religion. However, whether we believe the myth or not, it does not diminish the evidence we have and can discern from the Bible. The myth concerns Nimrod, his alleged wife Semiramis and their son Tammuz. As we have already seen the biblical description of Nimrod associates him with rebellion against God. While it does not say that he built the Tower of Babel, it does say that he built a kingdom centred on Babel and then went on to extend this kingdom around Nineveh.

The myth has many variants, but in outline it states that Nimrod ruled as king and with his wife founded a religious cult in which they were deified. When Nimrod died, perhaps murdered by his wife Semiramis, she ruled as queen in his stead. Many years later she became pregnant in mysterious circumstances and gave birth to a son, Tammuz,[4] around the time of the winter solstice. This miraculously conceived son was himself killed by a wild boar at the age of forty and then miraculously resurrected. He was said to be brought back to life through his mother's persistent tears from the time of his death until the early spring. His return to life came to be celebrated as the festival of Ishtar or Easter. Thus was born the myth of the mother and child and the resurrection of a divine son.[5]

Worldwide spread of pagan worship

The parallel aspects of worldwide pagan faiths, especially the idea of a mother-goddess, seem truly remarkable until we tie it in with Scripture. As we know from the story in *Genesis Chapter 11*, God came down to earth and confused human language in order to frustrate the people's idolatrous activities. This inevitably led to people groups with the same language moving away from Mesopotamia across the world, as they could no longer converse with their neighbours! Nevertheless they took their Babylonian pagan religion with them. If it is true (and it may not be) that the continents were not separated from a single land mass until the time of Peleg (see *Genesis 10:25* and *1 Chronicles 1:19*)[6] then this would explain why similar pagan religions were also found in places

like South and North America when European explorers discovered
the peoples of the 'New World' in the Middle Ages. They may well have
come from Babylon in Mesopotamia!

The spirit behind the myth

Readers may be wondering why the theme of a mother-goddess and
saviour son should appear in history long before the true Saviour,
Jesus Christ himself, appeared on earth. This is not difficult to explain
if we remember God's promises to Adam and Eve in *Genesis 3:15* and
if we also accept the satanic origin of the Babylonian and other pagan
religions. The descendants of Noah, himself a godly man, are likely
to have known what happened to Adam and Eve by oral tradition.
Satan certainly did, as he was there, having just entrapped the human
race through the sin of the first man and woman. This is how God
addressed Satan, the serpent:

> *I will put enmity between you and the woman, and between*
> *your offspring and her offspring; he shall bruise your head,*
> *and you shall bruise his heel.*
>
> *(Genesis 3:15)*

Many theologians agree that this is the prophetic beginning of God's
plan of salvation for the human race. Satan would have understood
that this involved a saviour being born to a woman sometime in
the future. He might have understood too that this Son needed to
be divine if he was to be free of the sin which now entrapped the
present and future human race. What better plan than to try and pre-
empt God by diverting human attention towards a false religion that
involved a deified mother and son. I stress that this is speculation,
but it does offer a possible explanation of the mother-son narrative in
many pagan religions.

   We should also be clear that the Bible does not validate this myth
of Nimrod and Semiramis in its fullness. For example, it does not even
mention that Nimrod was married. However, as we shall see shortly
it does refer to the Queen of heaven and it makes one mention of
Tammuz. It devotes several passages in the major prophets to the sins
of Babylon and its future downfall. It seems reasonable therefore to

argue that Babylon was the author of most, if not all of the world's pagan religions.

Pagan deities and the Queen of heaven

Not surprisingly the Bible devotes most attention to the pagan practices in the immediate vicinity of the Israelites, namely those of Canaan. This perhaps is the point to explain the similarities between Babylon and its pagan derivatives, ending with a more detailed look at the Canaanite religion. Before we do this it should be explained that many of these pagan religions are polytheistic – having many gods. This confuses the issue, but the male *sun/sky god* and the mother *moon/earth goddess* are usually the dominant deities. This confusion of gods is what surprised the apostle Paul when he went to Athens (*Acts 17:16-34*).

We usually find the cult of a mother-goddess associated with male sun-god worship. This goddess may represent the moon or the earth as the relevant counterpart to the sun. Thus the Queen of heaven may be interchangeable with the moon goddess. In religions more devoted to nature she may become mother-earth or mother-nature, manifestations we see in modern times. While most sun deities are male and most moon deities are female, this is not universal. There are also sun-goddesses and moon-gods, which can make polytheistic religions still more confusing!

The female goddess is usually associated with a son who is also a god; statuettes of the deity frequently show a mother with a baby or child.[7] An additional feature is that the child was sometimes worshipped as both husband and son of the mother-goddess. This may have come from the legend that Semiramis claimed that Nimrod her husband was reincarnated as the son Tammuz. Nevertheless, a pattern can be seen across the world of mother and son worship. Where this is so the mother holds a pre-eminent role, either being equal to or eclipsing the role of the son. This would again suit Satan's purpose in deflecting attention from the true Son, Jesus Christ, when he eventually appeared on earth. This emphasis on the mother has found expression in modern times in some Christian circles who believe that God should be addressed as 'Mother' and not 'Father', despite the clear statement of Scripture that God is our Father. Examples of these mother and son deities are given in Appendix 4.

Canaanite religion

The influence of Canaanite idolatry on the Israelites reads like an on-going headache for God through much of the Old Testament. In God's eyes this pagan derivative from Babylon had become a thoroughly depraved religion. Its most despicable practice was the sacrifice of children by fire to the god Molech. It was an abomination to God and he gave the Israelites three instructions, in all of which they failed. They were to destroy or expel the people of the land of Canaan as they took possession of it; they were not to intermarry with its inhabitants; and they were resolutely to refuse to indulge in any of their idolatrous practices (see *Exodus 23:30-33* and *34:11-16*). The Israelites ended up cohabiting with some of the Canaanite tribes, they did from time to time intermarry, but worst of all they fell into idolatry, adopting many of the practices of this false religion.

The principal male god of the Canaanites was Baal and his female goddess Ashtoreth (Astarte). The Canaanite practices included:

Sun and moon worship

Astrology

Sorcery

Child sacrifice to the god Molech

Cult prostitution

Interestingly these are all reflected in the Bible's many and strong rebukes to Babylon. *Isaiah Chapter 47* is revealing as a critique of the Babylonian religion. Babylon is referred to as a woman (as a virgin daughter) and Isaiah predicts the fall of this woman:

> *Come down and sit in the dust, O virgin daughter of Babylon;*
> *sit on the ground without a throne...*
>
> (Isaiah 47:1)

O daughter of the Chaldeans; for you shall no more be called the mistress of kingdoms.

(Isaiah 47:5)

As we shall see shortly, some of these verses are very similar to those in *Revelation Chapters 17* and *18*.

It is clear that Israel was involved in Babylonian pagan worship and not only that of Canaan. There is one revealing verse in Ezekiel (*Ezekiel 8:14*) where one of the abominations revealed in a vision to the prophet was the act of women weeping for Tammuz. We also find Jeremiah (in *Chapter 44*) addressing the Judeans who had disobeyed God and gone to Egypt to escape the Babylonians under Nebuchadnezzar: in particular he spoke against the women who openly defied the word of the Lord by declaring that they would continue to worship the Queen of heaven. A few verses after the reference to Tammuz, the Spirit of God revealed to Ezekiel an even greater abomination: men with their backs to the Temple (and thus to the Holy of Holies) worshipping the sun!

God's judgement of Babylon

Thus, although we have no direct confirmation of the myth relating to Nimrod, Semiramis and Tammuz, we do have firm evidence that Babylon was at the centre of a pagan religion, opposed to God. *Isaiah 47* is again revealing: the object of God's anger is a woman (goddess) with great evil power.

... in spite of your many sorceries and the great power of your enchantments. You felt secure in your wickedness...

(Isaiah 47:9-10)

This 'woman' despite her self-confidence will be brought low in a day:

Now therefore hear this, you lover of pleasures, who sits securely, who say in your heart, "I am, and there is no-one besides me; I shall not sit as a widow or know the loss of children": These two things shall come to you in a moment, in one day; the loss of children and widowhood shall come upon you in full measure, in spite of your many sorceries and the great power of your enchantments.

(Isaiah 47:8-9)

What is fascinating is that similar words of destruction are spoken in *Revelation Chapter 18*:

... since in her heart she says, "I sit as a queen, I am no widow, and mourning I shall never see." For this reason her plagues will come in a single day, death and mourning and famine, and she will be burned up with fire; for mighty is the Lord God who has judged her.
  Alas! Alas! You great city, you mighty city, Babylon! For in a single hour your judgement has come.

(Revelation 18:7-8, 10)

Notice that Babylon is described as a city in the context of its destruction.

God has been very patient with *Mystery: Babylon*, which spawned so many variants of its pagan religion. Now, however, its day of reckoning has come, to both the city and its system of religion.

Babylon in the end-times

If we examine *Revelation Chapters 17* and *18* more closely we can discern a number of things. An angel explains to the apostle John what is happening. It is:

... the judgement of the great prostitute who is seated on many waters.

(Revelation 17:1)

'Many waters' is recognised by theologians as a metaphor for the Gentile nations (see *Revelation 17:15*). This pagan religion is worldwide and is described as a prostitute. Israel who was described as being married to God as his wife (*Isaiah 54:5-8*), was often described as a harlot when its people went after foreign gods. Unfaithfulness to God was equated with sexual immorality. This is not simply an analogy: Canaanite and other pagan religions celebrated the practice of sexual immorality with the temple or cult prostitutes as part of their worship, a satanic perversion pure and simple!

It seems that by this time in the Tribulation we have this false religion, *Mystery: Babylon*, working very closely with the political and economic powers, possibly those of a world government. The woman is described as sitting on a scarlet beast full of blasphemous names (*Revelation 17:3*). This beast is none other than the Antichrist and his associated governments (10 horns equivalent to 10 kings, see *Revelation 13:1*). I will leave out the symbolic description of what happens to these kings (*Revelation 17:7-13*), except to say that some Bible expositors consider *verse 13*, where they hand over their power to the beast, as indicative of a unified world government.

What I now want to draw the reader's attention to is *Revelation 17:16*, where it says that the Antichrist and his associated kings will come to hate the prostitute and this will be the downfall of *Mystery: Babylon*. It actually says in *verse 17* that it is God who will put it into the hearts of the beast and the kings to carry out his purpose. God deals with one satanic creation (pagan religion) by using another (the Antichrist) before finally destroying this second one at the Second Advent of his Son, Jesus Christ.

The true nature of Mystery: Babylon

There are two further things to draw to the attention of the reader in these two chapters about *Mystery: Babylon*:

1. The woman is said to be drunk with the blood of the saints, the blood of the martyrs of Jesus (*Revelation 17:6*). By this stage of the Tribulation the gloves are off! There is no place for the believer in Christ who is now in mortal danger from this renegade religion.

2. Parts of this religion, perhaps in certain places in the world, may still have a veneer of Christianity. *Revelation 18:4-5* says:

Come out of her my people, lest you take part in her sins,
lest you share in her plagues; for her sins are heaped high as
heaven, and God has remembered her iniquities.

People who come to faith in Christ during the Tribulation (or the Church
going through the Tribulation) are warned to avoid the contamination
associated with this false religion.

Christian writers down the ages have attempted to identify *Mystery:*
Babylon with the Catholic Church. It is certainly true that during the
Middle Ages it martyred many true believers in Christ. It also adopted
some of Babylon's pagan practices, principally the 'mother and child',
but I do not think we should push this analogy too far. Despite its
failings, the Catholic Church today has many believers with a personal
faith in Christ. In my view it is still a Christian, not a pagan religion.

However, we may be approaching a time when the established
Christian churches, Catholic, Orthodox and Protestant, will feel
pressured to join forces with pagan and other religions to form one
worldwide religious body. It would no doubt be argued that religious
unity was a compromise worthwhile in the interests of co-operation
and world peace. There is already pressure for one-world government,
labouring under the simplistic human view that such a government
would be a major step towards solving the world's problems. Born-
again believers (if not already raptured) would oppose such a move,
but they would be a minority in the nominal Christian church. This
kind of unity might seem a pipe dream at the moment. Some religions,
such as Islam, would resist such a move initially, but the process could
happen incrementally.

What is clear is that if Christians find themselves in such an apostate
church or if they come to faith in one then it would be imperative
for them to leave it. Otherwise they might ultimately find themselves
worshiping the Antichrist with dire consequences for their eternal
destiny! (See *Revelation 14:9-11*).

The important thing to understand is that whether Christian
denominations join it or not, this end-times church will at heart be
a pagan religion. Its manifestations may vary in different parts of the
world due to different cultural and religious influences, but it will be
pagan. It will not simply be an apostate Christian church. To hold the

historical view of some Protestant denominations that this final church will be a reprobate Catholic Church is to miss the pagan nature of *Mystery: Babylon.*

Conclusion

Thus in *Revelation Chapters 17* and *18,* we have the downfall of *Mystery: Babylon.* This pagan religion founded so long ago in Babylon, based on rebellion to the one true God, and mother of so many false religions, will finally meet its end. The whole tone in heaven is one of: "about time too!" The voices in heaven do not hide their satisfaction (*Revelation 18:6-7*).

Modern Babylon: which city?

That leaves one more question: will there also be a destruction of a literal city of Babylon? The language of *Revelation 18:9-24* certainly suggests so. The problem is that ancient Babylon has been a site of ruins for many centuries. The sudden destruction predicted by *Revelation Chapter 18* and the judgements of the prophets (Isaiah and Jeremiah) suggest a desolation that does not match the history of Babylon's decline and fall. Its decline was slow and it survived as a place of residence into the early centuries AD. It is true that the ruins of ancient Babylon could match the description of Isaiah as a desolate haunt of wild animals and satyrs (demons) (see *Isaiah 13:21-22*), but nothing like the one-hour destruction of *Revelation Chapter 18* has yet happened to it.

Alternatively, could this destruction apply to another city? The candidate most commonly suggested is Rome, as a modern counterpart to ancient Babylon. Certainly ships could see the rising smoke of its destruction (*Revelation 18:17-18*). However, we are into the realm of speculation and there is no merit in trying to determine, either that a literal Babylon is rebuilt, or some other city has now become its modern namesake. What is clear, however, is that Babylon the religion is finally finished!

NOTES

1. The Internet has numerous articles on this subject covering the many practices associated with both Easter and Christmas. Before rushing to dispense with these Christian festivals it is worth reflecting on why we celebrate them. We celebrate them to honour the Lord Jesus Christ, not their origins in pagan history. However, some Christians take a stricter view. It is worth exploring the Internet for articles on how Christians perceive this issue.

2. It should be explained that chronologically Chapters 10 and 11 of Genesis almost certainly run concurrently. This is made clear by the fact that *Genesis 10:5* describes Japheth's descendants as spreading outwards each with their own language. This could not have happened before the Tower of Babel described in *Chapter 11.*

3. *Isaiah Chapters 13, 21, 47; Jeremiah Chapter 51.*

4. Nimrod reincarnated as his son.

5. Many practices associated with Christmas and Easter are said to originate with this pagan myth. Examples would include the evergreen decorated tree, the Lenten fast, the Easter egg and Easter bunny.

6. Peleg means division. Traditionally, Christians have tended to believe that these verses refer to the 'Patriarchal' tribal division of the earth and not to a physical division of the land which they believe happened at the time of Noah's Flood. More recently, however, some Bible students have surmised that the verses refer to the separation of the different continents from one landmass, sometimes called Pangaea. It would explain why so many tribes were dispersed across the world onto so many different islands and landmasses. It is nevertheless supposition, not an established fact.

7. A Google search of the Internet, "images of mother and son deities" will bring up examples from across the world.

10 *THE MILLENNIUM*

Having argued that the Millennium is a real span of time lasting 1000 years and that it follows the return of Christ at the end of the Tribulation, it is now necessary to say something about it: about its purpose and its nature. The hope of the apostles concerning the Kingdom in *Acts 1:6* was correct. The Kingdom will be restored to Israel.

It should be said at the outset that the Millennium is not the same as the new heaven and new earth that are described in *Revelation Chapters 21* and *22*. The Millennium precedes this time. We can be certain of this for two reasons:

1. Sin and the possibility of sin are still present during this time. Sin and death will only be abolished in eternity.

2. The apostle Paul tells us that Jesus:

   ... delivers the kingdom to God the Father after destroying every rule and every authority and power. For he must reign until he has put all his enemies under his feet.

   (1 Corinthians 15:24-25)

It is clear that Jesus is still very much in charge in the Millennium and that Satan has not finally been dispatched to hell.

The purpose of the Millennium

We can discern several purposes for the Millennium:

1. Jesus Christ will appear at his Second Advent as a king to rule his kingdom, in contrast to his first appearance as the suffering servant (see *Isaiah Chapters 52* and *53*).

2. Israel will receive the fullness of the promises inherent in the Abrahamic, Davidic and New Covenants (*Jeremiah 31:31-34*) of the Old Testament. It will be the pre-eminent nation on earth.

3. The earth will experience a time of righteous government. Mankind will see how government and relationships should have been managed, had the human race not been under the curse of sin.

4. This will be facilitated by the locking up of Satan and his army of fallen angels and evil spirits for the duration of the Millennial Kingdom.

5. The sin nature will still be present in mortal men and women born in the Millennium (as distinct from the resurrection saints who are said to be present and to rule with Christ). The release of Satan right at the end of the Millennium will serve to expose this nature since he succeeds in fomenting rebellion against King Jesus and his kingdom. It is God's final exposure of man's fallen nature. Satan may foment rebellion, but sin is an inborn problem for the human race until it is dealt with through the acceptance of Christ's sacrificial death on our behalf.

What will the Millennium be like?

Although *Revelation 20:1-10* defines the length of the Millennium there is very little detail in the passage as to what it will be like. For this we have to go to the Old Testament where there are many passages that refer to the Millennium without specifying its duration. These are found particularly in Isaiah and Ezekiel, but also in Jeremiah and some of the minor prophets. Many of these passages talk of a rejuvenated Jerusalem and the presence of God, passages which are difficult to understand if they are not referring to this period. Ezekiel, however, is very practical. He describes the restoration of the Jews, the allocation of the land to the twelve tribes and the foreigners living among them and the geographical layout of Jerusalem and its surroundings. He goes on to give a very detailed account of the construction of the Millennial Temple and its functioning. There are many aspects of the Millennium, but we shall concentrate on the major ones, to give a flavour of this time on earth.

These themes are:

The presence of the Lord Jesus Christ

The significance of Jerusalem and the Temple

The inhabitants of the Millennium

General aspects of the kingdom

Closure of the Millennium

The presence of the Lord Jesus Christ

We have seen that Jesus makes his second visit to earth to bring the Tribulation to a close. He deals with his enemies arrayed against him at Armageddon and dispatches the Antichrist and his false prophet to their eternal destiny in the lake of fire (see *Revelation 19:11-21*). He then sets about renovating the earth and preparing it for his Millennial reign. As we can imagine from the destruction that has happened in the Tribulation, this is no small task. We are not told much about this restoration, but Jesus does not do it single-handed! He will be present on earth as God-Man and in the office of reigning King. He will dwell here as a human being with a governing structure that would seem to be drawn from both resurrected saints and mortal humans. This is very much a time of demonstrating how human governance and living should have happened on earth, had Adam and Eve not sinned.

Although Jesus will have demonstrated his supernatural powers at the battle for Armageddon, I think we can expect life on earth during the Millennium to be natural rather than supernatural. We know that Jesus can turn water into wine (*John Chapter 2*) but I think we can safely take it that wine in the kingdom will be produced by the natural fermentation of grapes! (See *Amos 9:14.*) Nevertheless, there are passages of Scripture which suggest that agriculture will thrive and be especially fruitful during this time (for example *Isaiah 35:1-2* and *27:6*).

Jesus inherits the throne of David

The Old Testament makes clear that Jesus will inherit the throne of David. Government will be upon his shoulders and he will execute justice and righteousness. This is summed up in the well-known passage from *Isaiah 9:6-7.* We mostly remember the start of the passage:

> *For unto us a child is born, unto us a son is given...*
>
> > *(Isaiah 9:6 KJV)*

However, the rest of the passage describes his rule and kingship, something that did not happen on his first visit to earth. These characteristics are emphasised in other scriptures such as *Jeremiah 23:5-6; 33:14-17* and *Luke 1:30-33. Zechariah 14:9* emphasises that he will be king over all the earth, not just Israel.

Jesus' rule will be righteous, but it will also be firm. His reign will be a theocracy, not a democracy! Describing the woman (Israel) in *Revelation Chapter 12,* the Bible says:

> *She gave birth to a male child, one who is to rule all the nations **with a rod of iron**, but her child was caught up to God and to his throne...*
>
> > *(Revelation 12:5;* see also *19:15)* [emphasis added]

The prophet Micah says:

> *For out of Zion shall go forth the law, and the word of the Lord from Jerusalem. He shall judge between many peoples, and shall decide for strong nations far away...*
>
> > *(Micah 4:2-3)*

King Jesus will certainly not be a passive monarch!

The sin nature will continue in mortal man during this time and it will be necessary for regulations and laws which will emanate from the King's government and which will have to be strictly obeyed. The character of his rule is further enhanced in Isaiah:

> *There shall come forth a shoot from the stump of Jesse, and a branch from his roots shall bear fruit. And the Spirit of the Lord shall rest upon him, the Spirit of wisdom and understanding, the Spirit of counsel and might, the Spirit of knowledge and the fear of the Lord. And his delight shall be in the fear of the Lord. He shall not judge by what his eyes see, or decide disputes by what his ears hear, but with righteousness he shall judge the poor, and decide with equity for the meek of the earth; and he shall strike the earth with the rod of his mouth, and with the breath of his lips he shall kill the wicked. Righteousness shall be the belt of his waist, and faithfulness the belt of his loins.*
>
> *(Isaiah 11:1-5)*

The significance of Jerusalem and the Temple

Jerusalem will be the seat of government and the centre of the world. The prophets are full of God's love for and interest in Jerusalem. Many believers see these descriptions of Jerusalem as poetic rather than realistic, and this is because many references *are not understood unless seen in the context of the Millennium.*

One of the reasons for this is that God's Temple and holy city are described as being on a very high mountain. For example, Ezekiel is taken in a vision and *"set down on a very high mountain"* where he sees the city (*Ezekiel 40:1-4*). The prophet Micah says:

> *It shall come to pass **in the latter days** that the mountain of the house of the Lord shall be established as the highest of the mountains, and it shall be lifted up above the hills; and peoples shall flow to it, and many nations shall come, and*

say: "Come, let us go up to the mountain of the Lord, to the
house of the God of Jacob, that he may teach us his ways and
that we may walk in his paths."

(Micah 4:1-2) [emphasis added]

The clear message here is that Jerusalem and the Temple will sit on a
very high mountain, possibly the highest in the world (or at least in the
Middle East).[1] This hardly corresponds to what we know of Jerusalem
today. Mount Zion, Mount Moriah and the Mount of Olives are high
hills but hardly warrant mountain status. They nowhere near match
Mount Hermon, Israel's present highest mountain in the north of
the country.

We have seen that the earth will experience massive geological
changes during the Tribulation. The last earthquake of the Tribulation
corresponding to the seventh bowl judgement (*Revelation 16:17-20*) is
so great that it exceeds all previous earthquakes. Existing mountain
ranges may be altered and flattened at this time. The passage in
Revelation says:

And every island fled away, and no mountains were to be
found.

(Revelation 16:20)

It is not unreasonable to suppose that the new geological status of
Jerusalem is created at this time. It is clear from the texts that God
wants Jerusalem and the Temple to be on a high citadel in honour of
his Son, the King.

Ezekiel's Temple

This is not the book to discuss the details of Jerusalem and especially
the Temple. They are presented in great detail by the prophet Ezekiel:

The Temple (*Ezekiel Chapters 40-46*)

Jerusalem, its surroundings and the division of land (*Ezekiel*
Chapters 47-48)

Most of us need help in understanding both the layout of Jerusalem
and that of the Temple. I suggest a search on the Internet, but I

can recommend one website based on Paul Jablonski's book *Sons to Glory*, as this presents good maps and a well-constructed model of the Temple.[2] Some readers will know that Ezekiel describes the reinstitution of animal sacrifices in this Temple. I have explained the conflicting views on this in Appendix 5.

Ezekiel's Temple will be different from both the First Temple (Solomon's) and the Second Temple (Zerubbabel's, later expanded by Herod) in a number of ways. It will be larger than both. It will not have the Ark of the Covenant present in Solomon's Temple, which was lost at the time of the exile to Babylon,[3] but it will have the Shekinah glory of God which was missing from the Second Temple.

Ezekiel writes of his vision:

> *As the glory of the Lord entered the Temple by the gate facing east, the Spirit lifted me up and brought me into the inner court; and behold, the glory of the Lord filled the Temple.*
>
> *(Ezekiel 43:4-5)*

> *... and he said to me, "Son of man, this is the place of my throne and the place of the soles of my feet, where I will dwell in the midst of the people of Israel forever."*
>
> *(Ezekiel 43:7)*

The inhabitants of the Millennium

There is some confusion as to who will populate the Millennium. This arises largely through uncertainty as to when particular groups of believers will be resurrected. I will try to keep to what we can reasonably deduce from the scriptures.

We have seen that the Tribulation will lead to much loss of life among both Jews and Gentiles. It does seem that despite this terrible time (or even because of it), there will be widespread evangelism and many will turn to a saving faith in Christ. *Revelation Chapter* 7 suggests the 144,000 Jewish males sealed to God may play a major part in this evangelism. Many of those who turn to Christ will lose their lives at the hands of the Antichrist.

After the time of Christ's confrontation with his enemies at Armageddon, the following groups of people will enter the Millennium:

1. Resurrected saints (Jewish and Gentile) who have returned to earth with Christ at his Second Advent. Several passages indicate that Jesus returns with his angels (*Matthew 24:29-31; 2 Thessalonians 1:7*), but others refer to him returning with the saints (*1 Thessalonians 3:13; Jude 14-15*).[4]

   We know that resurrected saints will be on earth during the Millennium because several scriptures indicate that they have responsibility over the nations and in making judgements.

   The one who conquers and who keeps my works until the end, to him I will give authority over the nations...

   (Revelation 2:26)

   Other passages include: *Luke 19:16-19* and *1 Corinthians 6:2-3*. In *Matthew 19:28* the apostles are told they will judge the twelve tribes of Israel.

2. Mortals (Jews and Gentiles) who have survived the Tribulation. By this time the surviving Jews will have had their epiphany and recognised Jesus as their Messiah. They will all go into the Millennium.

The judgement of the sheep and goats from among the nations

The situation for Gentiles who survive the Tribulation, however, is not so simple. They will experience a judgement and separation before Christ himself and it is a salutary one. It reminds us that God takes very seriously how the Gentile nations treat the Jews. The passage of Scripture in question (*Matthew 25:31-46*) is a long one and we cannot avoid its conclusions. Both the context (*Matthew Chapters 24* and *25*) and the content indicate that this judgement relates to the Second Advent of Christ and the start of his Millennial Kingdom. All the nations are gathered before Jesus[5] and he separates the people into goats and sheep. The goats go to his left and the sheep to his right. The basis of the judgement is simple: it is how the Gentiles treated the Jews (Jesus' brothers) during their recent history. The time in question is the second half of the Tribulation when the Jews will have been hunted down by the Antichrist, but it could also apply to recent history before the Tribulation. Gentiles will have made decisions to help and protect Jews or to ignore or expose them. If they chose to help them then they will have risked their lives.

The helpers (*sheep*) are graciously ushered into the kingdom, some not realising that it was their good heart towards the Jews that has earned them this privilege (*verse 34-40*). Those who spurned the Jews or were active anti-Semites (*goats*) will suffer death and eternal separation from God (*verses 41-46*).

The beginning of the Millennium

There are lots of unanswered questions about the start of the Millennium. The world's population will have been greatly reduced by the preceding time of trouble. We can expect several hundred million mortal Jews and Gentiles to enter the Millennial Kingdom.[6] It is a reasonable supposition that all the Jews will have recognised their Messiah and accepted his salvation. The Gentiles (sheep) are blessed by God, and in view of what has just happened in Christ's judgement of the nations, are also likely to recognise the Messiah as their Saviour, at some point in the future if not there and then.

The continuing problem of sin

In view of both Jewish and Gentile recognition of Jesus as their Messiah or Saviour, it is reasonable to ask why there will be a continuing problem of sin for mortal people who enter the Millennial Kingdom. That sin will continue into the Millennium is clear from Isaiah:

> *And the sinner a hundred years old shall be accursed.*
> *(Isaiah 65:20)*

And also from Revelation:

> *And when the thousand years are ended, Satan will be released from his prison and will come out to deceive*

*the nations that are at the four corners of the earth, Gog
and Magog, to gather them for battle... [against the saints
and Jerusalem].*

(Revelation 20:7-8) [comment added]

While those entering the Kingdom may acknowledge King Jesus
and what he has done for them, those born to these mortals will
not necessarily do so. Christians today are only too well aware that
their children may not follow in their beliefs.[7] This will also be true of
the Millennial children. The sin nature is still there and Satan's final
deception will bring it out for all to see.

Resurrected believers in the Millennium

It is difficult in this life to comprehend how resurrected saints will live
alongside mortal human beings in the Millennial Kingdom. However,
the scripture is clear: they will be there and they will have governing
responsibilities in the Kingdom under King Jesus. Some writers think
we need a glorified body because we return to earth and that such a
body is not needed in heaven. My own view is that a glorified body is
part of our redemption as believers whether in heaven or on earth. I
can well imagine that we may 'commute' between the two domains as
we carry out our responsibilities.

General aspects of the Millennial Kingdom

It is very important to be clear that the Millennial Kingdom is not
the same as the new heaven and new earth described in *Revelation
Chapters 21* and *22*. Isaiah seems to be referring to this in *Chapter 65*
when he says:

*For behold, I create new heavens and a new earth, and the
former things shall not be remembered or come into mind.*

(Isaiah 65:17)

The past is forgotten. However, the rest of the chapter (*verses 18-25*)
is clearly about the Millennial Kingdom. There is no way that we can

countenance sin or the sin nature in the new heaven and earth. Yet sin and death are clearly mentioned in this passage (*verse 20*). Nevertheless, there will be enormous beneficial changes in the Millennial Kingdom, some of which we will now examine.

We have already seen that the earth will have experienced enormous geological and topographical changes. As we might expect when Christ himself reigns on earth there will be huge improvements to the environment, the way we live, agricultural productivity and so on.

One of the first things to happen is the banishment of war and the manufacture of armaments. In the famous passage from Isaiah it says;

> *For out of Zion shall go the law, and the word of the Lord from Jerusalem. He shall judge between the nations, and shall decide disputes for many peoples; and they shall beat their swords into ploughshares, and their spears into pruning-hooks; nation shall not lift up sword against nation, neither shall they learn war any more.*
>
> *(Isaiah 2:3-4)*

This is repeated in *Micah Chapter 4*.

There will be major changes to nature. In *Romans Chapter 8* the apostle Paul speaks of the whole creation groaning and that it will be set free from its bondage to corruption. This may not happen in its entirety until the new heavens and earth, but we may have the first fruits of this release in the Millennium.

In Isaiah it says:

> *"The wolf and the lamb shall graze together; the lion shall eat straw like the ox, and dust shall be the serpent's food. They shall not hurt or destroy in all my holy mountain," says the Lord.*
>
> *(Isaiah 65:25)*

This would imply that carnivorous animals become vegetarian. Of this we cannot be sure, but we can declare that the environment will become a safe place and work will be a pleasure.

They shall build houses and inhabit them; they shall plant vineyards and eat their fruit. They shall not build and another inhabit; they shall not plant and another eat; for like the days of a tree shall the days of my people be, and my chosen shall long enjoy the work of their hands.

(Isaiah 65:21-22)

Children will survive and live long lives:

No more shall there be in it an infant who lives but a few days...

(Isaiah 65:20)

They shall not labour in vain or bear children for calamity...

(Isaiah 65:23)

Our knowledge from Scripture concerning the Millennium is limited, but we can tell that it will be a time of blessing on earth.

Closure of the Millennium

This time of blessing and peace comes to a close with the Satan-inspired rebellion already mentioned (*Revelation 20:7-10*). This is quickly dealt with by God and Satan is sent to his final abode, the lake of fire. The Bible then moves, presumably in heaven, to the resurrection of the unsaved dead and the Great White Throne judgement (*Revelation 20:11-14*). This is followed by the creation of the new heaven and earth, where sin, death, tears and sadness are no more.

I shall not examine this further as it is not part of the current study. Instead I will direct the reader to the closing chapters of *Revelation, Chapters 21* and *22.*

NOTES

1. This does not mean that Jerusalem has to be as high as Mount Everest. Such height would make it uninhabitable. The last earthquake of Revelation *(Revelation 16:17-20)* clearly causes enormous topographical changes to the earth, and the future of Jerusalem must be seen in this context.

2. Paul Jablonski's model of the Ezekiel Temple:
    <http://www.sonstoglory.com/ThirdTempleEzekielsMillennialTemple.htm>
    However, I should say that I do not agree with his views on the Tribulation.

3. Legend has it that the ark was hidden by Jeremiah in the caves under Jerusalem. This would seem to be born out by the second book of *Maccabees Chapter 2:5*, which although an apocryphal book, is also historical.

4. The Greek words used for angels and saints are different: confusion probably arises because *saints* are sometimes described as *holy ones*, which could apply to both angels and saints. Almost certainly angels and saints are present.

5. We are not told how this will happen in practice.

6. In absolute terms this is a large number, but relative to the pre-Tribulation population of the earth it will be small. The reality is that we cannot assess the actual number.

7. However, Christians do have a very effective weapon – they can and should, pray for their children!

11 *WHAT DOES THE FUTURE HOLD?*

W̲e̲ come now to the question of when this will all happen. I do not suggest that we should be looking for dates, but I think we should be aware of seasons. This is not an academic question. If the time of Christ's return is 500 years away then we do not need to address the matter, but if it is measured in decades then Christians need to take it seriously.

Believers have awaited the Lord's return from soon after the birth of the Church. Biblical expressions such as *the things that must soon take place (Revelation 1:1)* heightened believers' expectations of the Lord's early return. However, God's understanding of 'soon' does not have to equate with ours.

Many Christians feel that God has built a time-scale into the creation and redemption of the human race which it ought to be possible to decipher. This is not an unreasonable expectation because God has built numbers into much of the Bible. It would be surprising if underlying the seeming randomness of so much in the universe, the Creator had not done this. After all, the beauty and precision of mathematics is God's creation.

However, deciphering it is a different matter and has led to many cul-de-sacs and false dates. The reality is that there may not be an underlying time scale and if there is one, God may not want us to uncover it this side of heaven.

The principal approaches have been:

1. To base man's creation and redemption on the 'perfect' figure of 7000 years.

2. To tie such a pattern in with the Jewish feasts.

or

3. To base it on figures given in the book of Daniel concerning the
    70 weeks.

Most Christians believe that we cannot discern the time of his Second
Advent because of Jesus' words:

> But concerning that day and hour no one knows, not even
> the angels of heaven, nor the Son, but the Father only.
>
> *(Matthew 24:36)*

Some Christians on the other hand believe that this applies to the date
of the Rapture. They argue that this does not preclude the possibility
that we may be able to discern the date of Christ's Second Advent.

Signs for the end of the age

I do not propose to pursue this idea, but I do think we can discern
the seasons. Jesus himself gave us an indication of this in his Olivet
discourse when the disciples asked him about the sign of his coming
and the close of the age (*Matthew 24:3*). Jesus listed various things
that would happen (*verse 6*), but these would not indicate the end. For
example he said the disciples would hear of wars and rumours of wars.
In *verses 7-8* however, Jesus began to list things which could indicate
that the end of the age had begun:

> For nation will rise against nation, and kingdom against
> kingdom, and there will be famines and earthquakes
> in¹ various places. All these are but the beginning of the
> birth pains.
>
> *(Matthew 24:7-8)*

In *Luke 21:11* the word *pestilences* (disease epidemics) is added to
famines. Thus we have the following signs with which the close of the
age will **commence**:

1. Wide scale warfare

2. Famines and disease epidemics

3. Earthquakes

Turning first to famines, epidemics and earthquakes I think it is important to appreciate that it is not a simple task to assess whether we have now reached a time of absolute increase in these events or just a perception that there are more of them. Some Christian writers state that we have now reached a time of more frequent disasters, but a search of the Internet reveals that there are competing claims. Scientific assessments make it less certain. Let us consider the factors we must bear in mind with earthquakes.

1. The world's population has increased dramatically in the last 100 years. This means that more people are affected by earthquakes when they do happen.

2. Seismic and scientific recording of earthquakes has only been possible since the early 1900's. This has become greatly refined over the last century.[2] Today we can measure earthquakes that people in Jesus's time or even up to the 1800's would not have been aware of.

3. Since the invention of the telegraph in the 1850's communications have expanded at a colossal rate. Little happens in the world today that we are not aware of within a few hours. In the past it might have taken weeks before news of an earthquake or other disaster arrived, or it may never have arrived.

Furthermore, an objective assessment would need to ask: Where does one draw the line at the size of the earthquake? Does one measure its size by loss of life and damage to infrastructure as would have been the case throughout most of history, or does one measure it on the modern seismic scale? Over what time span is one measuring the increase? Most of the measurement applies to the limited span of the twentieth century since this is the period of accurate seismographic measurement.

Turning to famines and epidemics, there have been some horrific famines in the twentieth century.[3] This same century has also seen some terrible epidemics, such as the influenza pandemic of 1918-21.

Some historians might argue that these famines were matched by those in history. They might also argue that the epidemics were easily matched by the Justinian plague of the sixth century AD or the Black Death in the Middle Ages, in the way these plague decimated the population.

The reader can see that it is not easy to make an objective assessment as to whether such natural disasters are now more frequent. However, for the reasons given, we are much more aware of these events when they do occur and this is what Jesus may have meant in his Olivet discourse.

World wars

Turning to the third sign we may have a more definitive answer. In the passage from *Matthew 24:6-8* Jesus makes a distinction between wars and rumours of wars on the one hand, and nation rising against nation, and kingdom rising against kingdom on the other. Arnold Fruchtenbaum makes a convincing case[4] for arguing that the first worldwide conflict, World War I and its extension World War II, fulfilled this latter description of nations and kingdoms rising against each other. There had been many wars throughout history, but never a war on a world scale. This scale was true of both world wars as nations and empires from across the globe were involved. He also argues that both wars were significant in Jewish history. World War I gave impetus to the growth of the Zionist Movement through the defeat of the Ottoman Empire and the issue of the Balfour Declaration, while World War II led to the re-establishment of the Jewish state. The reason Dr Fruchtenbaum argues for this as a sign to the start of the end of the age is that the expression: "*nation against nation and kingdom against kingdom*" is a Hebrew idiom for a world war. He says that the Rabbis clearly taught that a worldwide conflict would signal the coming of the Messiah. Jesus' words modify this by saying that it would mark the **start** of the end of the age. He did not, of course say, how long this closure to the age would be.

Events which must precede the Tribulation

We have already seen that there must be a start to the close of the age as told by Jesus in *Matthew 24:7-8*. We have discussed the matter of famines, epidemics and earthquakes indicating that there has been a much greater awareness of these events in the last century than there was in previous history, without trying to define an absolute increase in these events. We have seen more definitively that worldwide conflict occurred for the first time in history with the two world wars in the first half of the twentieth century.

We now need to ascertain what other events must happen prior to the seven-year Tribulation (or day of the Lord) which will commence with the signing of a treaty between Israel and the Antichrist (*Daniel 9:27*). I will indicate signs which must definitely occur and those where there is less certainty.

Worldwide proclamation of the gospel

We will start with a sign which is sometimes overlooked by those Christians who think we are on the threshold of the Tribulation. Jesus said:

> *And this gospel of the kingdom will be proclaimed throughout the whole world as a testimony to all nations, and then the end will come.*
>
> (*Matthew 24:14*)

Despite the amazing spread of the gospel in the nineteenth and twentieth centuries this cannot be said to have happened yet. Organisations like the Joshua Project[5] argue that 42% of the world's people groups have not yet been reached with the gospel. Some Christians may want to argue that some of these people groups have been reached, but that the gospel did not take root or was actively rejected. Other Christians approach the issue from a different angle and argue that much of the remaining evangelisation will be completed in the first three and a half years of the Tribulation while the Antichrist is establishing himself in the Middle East.[6]

It seems to me that there is much to do before the Tribulation gets under way. Right at the end of the book I refer to a famous prophecy supposedly given by the evangelist Smith Wigglesworth. This refers to an end-times revival which will eclipse anything that has preceded it.

Re-establishment of the State of Israel

For the covenant of *Daniel 9:27* to be signed there must be a state which can act on the world stage, and which can sign treaties. This has happened. The modern State of Israel was founded on 15 May 1948. The prophet Isaiah says:

> *Who has heard such a thing? Who has seen such things? Shall a land be born in one day? Shall a nation be brought forth in one moment?*
>
> (Isaiah 66:8)

Given the dispersion of the Jews for over 2000 years this was a truly amazing event. It did literally come into existence in one day with the signing of the Declaration of Independence.

Jerusalem needs to be under Jewish control

This event has likewise happened. So much of the end-times are focused on Israel and its capital Jerusalem. We have also seen that the Temple must be rebuilt in order that there is a temple for the Antichrist to defile (*Daniel 9:27; Matthew 24:15*). Jerusalem came under Jewish control in June 1967 (with the Six-day War) as a consequence of Jordan breaking the armistice agreement between itself and Israel.[7]

The Temple has not been rebuilt and it is difficult to see this happening until the Antichrist signs the covenant with Israel and persuades or forces the Muslim nations to agree. If it were to happen this way then the Temple would have to be up and functioning in the first three and a half years of the Tribulation. However, this is speculation and it is worth remembering that God often surprises us in the way his plans work out.

The Antichrist must be revealed

This event has not yet happened. It means that Christians on earth at the time of his appearance will be able to recognise him, (although the world at large will not be aware of his biblical role). There are two reasons for this. First, it is stated in Scripture. The apostle Paul writes:

Let no one deceive you in any way. For that day will not come, unless the rebellion comes first, and the man of lawlessness is revealed, the son of destruction...

(2 Thessalonians 2:3)

The 'day' is referring to *the day of the Lord* in the previous verse. I have argued extensively (see Chapter 4) that the day of the Lord is to be equated with the Tribulation. If this is correct then the man of lawlessness must be revealed prior to the Tribulation.

The second reason is that Christians will know that the signing of the treaty between Israel and a significant world leader, heralds the Tribulation. The Antichrist cannot be a nonentity when he undertakes such a major task. He must be an existing world leader.

Unified world government

Some writers[8] believe that a unified world government followed by ten kingdoms must arise prior to the appearance of the Antichrist. This is based on the prophet Daniel's passage 7:23-24. I am not convinced by this reasoning because in a later passage, *Daniel 11:36-45* indicates that the Antichrist will have to wage war and subdue his enemies during the Tribulation (see *Daniel 11:40-44*), before he comes to a dominant position. It may not be until after this time that he will be secure enough to receive power from the ten kings and to institute a dictatorial world government. The information is not definitive enough to assert that there must be world government prior to the Tribulation. On the other hand it does seem more likely that the ten kings will already be on the world stage since Daniel states (*Daniel 7:24*) that another different king shall arise after them, a figure who is clearly identifiable with the Antichrist.

Wars associated with the Tribulation

This is a suitable point to discuss the wars that precede or are associated with the Tribulation. I do not propose to examine them in depth, mainly because there are diverse opinions as to what happens and when. A brief examination is necessary however, and will influence our view of pre-tribulation events.

Let us start with the wars which are definitely connected to the Tribulation. We have already seen that the death and destruction of the Tribulation will be immense. While this is partly due to God's judgemental natural disasters, most will be due to war.

Armageddon

The Battle of Armageddon is the most well known war. Even non-Christians have a sense of a final, apocalyptic war in history. This battle occurs right at the end of the Tribulation and can be read about in *Revelation 16:12-16* and *Revelation 19:11-21*. Astonishingly the Bible describes the Antichrist (the beast) and the kings of the earth assembling in Israel to make war against the Lord Jesus Christ himself (*Revelation 19:19*). I recognise that this could be symbolic of the Jews, as most of the assembled soldiers will not be aware of Christ's imminent arrival. Nevertheless, these will be strange times. The Antichrist and his false prophet will have displayed supernatural signs and wonders (*Revelation 13:11-15*) and Satan may well have given them prior knowledge of Christ's imminent arrival. In their arrogance they may think they can defeat him!

The Lord Jesus, on his return, makes short work of the battle. The Antichrist and the false prophet are captured and dispatched to the lake of fire (eternal hell), while the rest of the armies are destroyed by the Lord himself (*Revelation 19:21*). It would seem from the text that he destroys them with a word from his mouth.

Wars within the seven-year Tribulation

We have references at various points in the book of Revelation which point to hugely destructive wars. The first reference is in *Revelation Chapter 6* where the first four seals release the four *Horsemen of the Apocalypse* who are given the power of death through warfare and famine, leading to the death of one quarter of the earth's population. It is possible that the four horsemen are symbolic of the death and destruction throughout the Tribulation and that they encompass the more specific events described in later chapters. Many writers think they refer to separate events, but we cannot be entirely sure of this.

In *Revelation Chapters 8* and 9 we meet the specific warfare of the Trumpet judgements 1 and 6 (Trumpet 6 is sometimes called the second woe). Trumpet 1 with its references to hail and fire and the burning up of one third of the earth could easily be the description of nuclear war. Trumpet 6 releases a huge army of troops which is said to kill one third of mankind. Once again the description of this warfare sounds very like nuclear war.

If we now turn to *Daniel 11:40-45* we are given a more specific description of wars undertaken by the Antichrist. These seem to take place in the early part of the Tribulation when the Antichrist is consolidating his power. A series of battles is described with various kings involving great loss of life and destruction, but out of which the Antichrist emerges victorious.

These may be part of the wars we have just met in *Revelation Chapters 6, 8* and *9*. We cannot, however, be sure of this.

The war of Gog and Magog

We now come to the wars that possibly precede the Tribulation. The war of Gog and Magog seems to be an entirely separate war that is described in great detail in *Ezekiel Chapters 38* and *39*. *Ezekiel 38:8* clearly locates this war in the end-times.

Gog is a leader and he is described as being from the land of Magog, as well as being the prince of Meshech and Tubal. He is described as forming an alliance with other nations: Persia, Cush, Put, Gomer and Beth-togarmah who then attack an Israel resting securely in *"the land of unwalled villages"* (*Ezekiel 38:11*).[9] Gog and his allies will be utterly defeated and it seems that this will be due to God's direct intervention. One striking feature is that none of the nations listed in this war are existing Arab neighbours of Israel.

The problem with this war is where to place it. Some writers move it to the end of the Millennium and believe it is the final battle orchestrated by Satan after his release from the Abyss (*Revelation 20:7-9*). Gog and Magog are mentioned, but various factors make it unlikely that this is the war described in such detail in *Ezekiel Chapters 38* and *39*. At the end of the Millennium God dispatches his enemies very quickly by fire from heaven. He is about to wind up the old earth, and it seems out of keeping to describe the time taken to bury the dead and clear up the wreckage of war at this stage in history.

On the other hand there are problems if one tries to fit the war into the first half of the Tribulation. It would have to be right at the beginning, but the cleaning up could only last for half of the designated seven years (*Ezekiel 39:9*), since Israel is told by Jesus in the Olivet discourse (*Matthew Chapter 24*) to flee from the Antichrist at the midpoint of the Tribulation.

On reading Ezekiel's description of this war, it does seem that God has a very specific and public contention with Gog, the people of Magog and their allies. There is no mention of the Antichrist which would be surprising if the war belonged to the time of the Tribulation. We can be certain that Gog is not the Antichrist because Ezekiel mentions that he is killed in the war and buried in Israel (*Ezekiel 39:11*). This is one of several reasons the war of Gog and Magog cannot equate to the final battle of Armageddon.

This leaves one place to put the war and that is before the Tribulation. There is one difficulty with this, if the war were to happen any time soon. Israel is described as a land of unwalled villages, being at rest and dwelling securely (*Ezekiel 38:10-13*). It is very difficult to see how present day Israel fits this description at this particular time. It is a nation in constant readiness for war.

The war to exterminate Israel

These considerations about the war of Gog and Magog have led some writers to the view that there must be a further Middle East war that precedes that of Gog and Magog. Its proponents argue that it is prophesied in *Psalm 83* where the nations surrounding Israel say:

> *Come, let us wipe them out as a nation; let the name of Israel be remembered no more!*
>
> (Psalm 83:4)

The nations are said to be coveting the land and the Psalmist urges God to make an end to these people. It is then supposed (and this is pure speculation) that Israel is attacked, but that it vanquishes these nations, which leads to territorial expansion and the gain of natural resources. Israel is then able to dwell in peace and security as described in *Ezekiel Chapter 38*. This sets the scene for the alliance of Gog with other nations to covet these natural resources and attack Israel from the North.

I am not at all convinced by this argument. *Psalm 83* could be describing an on-going state of affairs that has existed since the re-establishment of Israel in 1948. It has been attacked several times by neighbouring Arab states, added to which groups like Hamas and Hezbollah and even the State of Iran have openly declared their desire to destroy the nation of Israel. *Psalm 83* does not say that God will respond to the urgings of the Psalmist.

As a consequence of all this we will have to leave the identity of the next major war in the Middle East open. However, I do acknowledge that the statement that Israel is dwelling securely in a land of unwalled villages creates an obstacle to the view that the war of Gog and Magog could be the next war, one which ushers in the Tribulation.

Summing up: the Tribulation wars

The Tribulation could be some way off and Israel could be involved in several further wars before it takes place. *Psalm 83* could be describing a war that is yet to take place and this could change the demography of the Middle East to create a time of security for Israel, which gives way to the war of Gog and Magog. However, it should be remembered that this is all supposition.

When the Tribulation arrives we do know that it will be ushered in by a covenant between Israel and the Antichrist to which other nations are likely to be party (willingly or unwillingly). We also know that there will be dramatic wars within the time frame of the Tribulation, though we cannot be sure where the specific war mentioned in *Daniel 11:40-45* fits into this timescale. We can be certain that the Tribulation will finish with the appearance of the Lord Jesus Christ and the defeat of the Antichrist and his armies at the battle of Armageddon.

We also know that the Millennium will end with the final battle initiated by Satan upon his temporary release from his place of incarceration. This will finally be 'the war to end all wars'.

Conclusion

We began this chapter by examining the signs for the start of the end-times, signs which Jesus called birth pangs. These included earthquakes, famines and pestilence and finally world war. While recognising that people were not in agreement as to whether we could objectively say there had been an increase in the first three signs, I suggested that the two world wars of the twentieth century were qualitatively different from all the wars which had preceded them. We could reasonably say therefore that these signified the start of the end of the age.

We then looked at signs which must or may precede the Tribulation and came to the conclusion that these were legitimate signs:

1. Worldwide proclamation of the gospel. While there are different views on when this will be complete, I argued that there is still work to do before the Tribulation commences.

2. The re-establishment of the State of Israel.

3. Jews must be in control of Jerusalem.

4. The Antichrist must be revealed.

5. The likelihood of a unified world government: I argued that this was a possibility but not a necessity.

6. Wars preceding the Tribulation. We looked at the biblical wars concerning this time, but did not come to a definite conclusion as to which wars were certain to precede this time of trouble.

In the last chapter we will take a brief look at further considerations which may give us some idea as to how close we could be to the end-times.

NOTES

1. Translations of the Greek word 'Kata' vary. My Interlinear Greek-English New Testament translates it as 'throughout' rather than 'in', implying there will be more earthquakes.

2. In 1931 there were about 350 seismographic stations; today there are 8000.

3. Notable events include the Russian famines of 1921 and 1931-33, those in China 1959-61, North Korea in the 1990's and Sub-Sahara Africa at various times.

4. Arnold Fruchtenbaum: Messianic Bible Study (MBS028) entitled *The Olivet Discourse* P.7-8.

5. See the Joshua Project website for its analysis: <joshuaproject.net/global_statistics>

6. Arnold Fruchtenbaum is one such person. He argues that the worldwide preaching of the gospel in *Matthew 24:14* will be conducted by the 144,000 Jews mentioned in *Revelation 7:1-8*. See Messianic Bible Study (MBS028) entitled *The Olivet Discourse* P.10-11. Whether his understanding is correct or not, I believe most Christian writers would consider that there is still much evangelisation to be done this side of the Tribulation.

7. See my book *Has God really finished with Israel?* P.26, Footnote 15.

8. See for example Arnold Fruchtenbaum's Messianic Bible Study (MBS038) *The Sequence of Pre-Tribulational Events* P.30.

9. There is general but not universal agreement on the modern identity of these nations, as a Google search of the Internet will reveal. Two passages show that the initial attack will come "from the uttermost parts of the north" (*Ezekiel 38:6* and *39:2*) and this does suggest that the alliance is centred around Russia, some of its former Soviet states, Persia, Turkey and also nations from the South such as Sudan (Cush) and North Africa (Put corresponds approximately to Libya). However, the various, usually well-argued opinions of different writers mean we cannot be sure of this.

12 *THE COMING YEARS*

We have examined events that must precede the Tribulation and seen that some have already occurred, some are still in the future and some are uncertain as to their timing. Are there any other signs that indicate we could be close to the events described in this book?

Since the establishment of the State of Israel in 1948 and in particular since the Six-day War in 1967 many Christians have focused their view of the end-times on what is happening in the Middle East. Some have tried unsuccessfully to predict events by reference to Jesus' story of the fig tree (*Matthew 24:32-34*) and the passing of a generation. Specific dates for the Rapture and/or the return of Christ have come and gone. We are well advised to avoid such date setting.

However, I do think we can discern signs which indicate that the end-times cannot be too long delayed. If this is so then we should begin to prepare for the return of Christ. Jesus' admonition to watch and pray (*Matthew Chapters 24* and *25*) is as valid today as it has ever been. Notwithstanding the need to take the gospel to many parts of the world (see previous chapter), the history of the Middle East in the twentieth century suggests we would be wise to expect the end-times to happen within decades rather than a longer interval of time. If we subscribe to the postmillennial or the amillennial view of Christ's return we may well lose that sense of urgency that belongs to the premillennial view. I do think we need to alert the world and those close to us that Christ's return could be soon.

I think there are two factors we should consider:

1. The possibility of nuclear war
2. The on-going Israel/Palestine conflict

The possibility of nuclear war

I grew up in the aftermath of the Second World War and during the development of the Cold War which ended in 1991 with the fall of communism and the break-up of the Soviet Union. We have been a fortunate generation in the West. We have not had to fight another world war. Ironically, the development of nuclear weapons by the USA and the USSR helped to keep the peace through a policy of *mutually assured destruction* (MAD was its apposite acronym!). Many localised wars were fought elsewhere in the world, but nuclear weapons were not deployed. Another factor was that the world had seen the destruction wrought by the two atomic bombs dropped on Japan at the end of the war. This protection during the Cold War depended on sane leadership which had seen the destruction of World War II, and on the non-proliferation treaty (effective from March 1970) which has restricted the spread of nuclear weapons for several decades. However, this restriction is now breaking down.[1] Despite these restraining influences in the second half of the twentieth century, the Cold War was a frightening time, especially for anyone who lived through the Cuban missile crisis of 1962. The world came to the very edge of nuclear devastation.

The situation today is very different and potentially more threatening. During the Cold War, many people in the West believed that despite the nuclear arms race between the United States and the USSR, the leaders would see reason and eventually agree to nuclear disarmament. This was the time of the marches to 'ban the bomb', such as those at Aldermaston in the United Kingdom. Arms limitation agreements did take place and the non-proliferation treaty has been relatively effective, but the genie was out of the bottle and the two world powers were never going to get rid of all their nuclear weapons, if only because of the threat that other nations might develop them.

Today the nuclear club includes India, Pakistan, Israel and North Korea as well as the initial five nations (see *Note 1*). Iran is soon likely to join them, and if and when that happens it is likely to start a nuclear arms race that will further destabilise the Middle East. The non-proliferation treaty could soon break down. Every smaller nation that joins the nuclear club increases the risk. Some of these nations are not constrained by the rational approach of the superpowers, the

USA and the USSR, during the Cold War. North Korea is a dangerous, unpredictable nation, Pakistan is politically unstable and Iran has indicated its wish to see Israel removed as a nation.[2]

Furthermore, there is the risk that small nuclear weapons could fall into the hands of ruthless terrorist groups such as Al-Qaeda who would have no qualms about blackmailing the western nations or even using the weapons.

God is in charge

Now as a Christian I know that God is in charge of the world's future and he will not allow Satan to pre-empt his plans. However, I have endeavoured to emphasise that the Tribulation is a time of God's wrath and judgement on a sinful world. It seems to me unlikely that he would have let mankind open the secrets of nuclear weapons if they were never going to be used.[3] Some of the descriptions in Revelation are reminiscent of the use of nuclear weapons and it seems inconceivable to me that the events of the Tribulation and the activities of the Antichrist would happen without the use of such weapons. The leaders of the allies in World War II (USA, Great Britain and the USSR) were extremely worried that Hitler's Germany might succeed in making such a weapon. There is not the slightest doubt that he would have used it or sought to dictate a peace by the threat of using it.

To sum up this argument: the existence of a nuclear club with unstable members and the fact that we may be on the threshold of a nuclear arms race in the Middle East, makes nuclear war a real possibility. Were this to happen, it seems likely that this would be one of the factors precipitating the end-times and the Tribulation.

The Israel/Palestine conflict

This is another flashpoint in the Middle East. For many years negotiators from the Western nations and the United Nations have sought to bring about a peace treaty that would have entailed a two-state solution to the Israeli/Palestinian conflict. Christians who support the re-establishment of Israel as a Jewish state and who follow the premillennial approach to the end-times know that this would not have been a permanent solution because of what will happen in the end-times, which has been the theme of this book.

However, I have always felt that it is right to support a political settlement to this dispute in the meantime. I think it is important for Christians to respect the rights of the Palestinians to live in the land as well as the Jews who return there. Some Christians do not share this view; they argue that Israel acquired the West Bank and Gaza in a defensive war and they should not give up the heartland of what was once ancient Israel (Judea and Samaria). The problem with this approach is that it never addresses the fact that several million Palestinian Arabs now live in the West Bank and Gaza. Had such an agreement been implemented, then we might have looked forward to a period of stability in the Middle East.

However, this seems increasingly unlikely. The talks in 2014 between the Israeli government and the Palestinian Authority broke down with little movement towards an agreement and little prospect that they will be revived. The Palestinian Authority appears to believe that it can get further recognition as a Palestinian state through various international agencies and that this will isolate Israel. There are even calls by some Palestinian leaders[4] to disband the Palestinian Authority. This would leave Israel to be responsible once again for an occupation which has gradually been relaxed in response to the Oslo Accords of 1993 and 1995. This would lead to a highly unstable situation in which extremist organisations could take over. This instability, leading perhaps to another Middle East war, is exactly the situation where Israel could seek the assistance of a charismatic world leader to resolve the issue and he could then turn out to be the Antichrist.

What might trigger the next major war in the Middle East involving Israel?

The failure to resolve the Israel/Palestine conflict is one source of instability, as we have just seen. However, there is another scenario which would almost certainly precipitate a war. Israel has made it abundantly clear to the world that it considers the acquisition of nuclear weapons by Iran a mortal threat to its existence. It feels that the United States and the other negotiating nations have been much too lenient towards Iran and have not obtained a secure agreement that Iran will halt nuclear weapons development.

Given this situation Israel may decide to launch a pre-emptive conventional weapons attack against Iran's nuclear facilities. This would provoke a response from Iran and outrage from the world. Nations like Russia might come to Iran's assistance and before the world wakes up Russia could be leading an attack against Israel in a war reminiscent of that described in *Ezekiel Chapters 38* and *39*.

Prophecy or possibility?

Let me emphasise that I am not making a prophecy; I am simply describing a possibility. Such possibilities have become more, not less likely in recent years. The point I am making with these two further considerations – the spread of nuclear weapons and the failure to resolve the Israel/Palestine conflict – is that the world and the Middle East in particular are becoming increasingly unstable. The current rapid expansion of ISIS, the extremist Islamic Caliphate, has further destabilised the region and drawn the Western nations back into conflict in the Middle East. History suggests that such instabilities do not last for any length of time. The First World War was supposed to be the 'war to end all wars', but in just over twenty years its unresolved issues led to the even more destructive Second World War.

We could be talking about the end-times unfolding in a matter of decades. We should at least think about it and prepare ourselves and our loved ones for this possibility. We need to strengthen our relationship with Jesus through our prayer life, our study of God's Word, the Bible and through our Christian activities. Furthermore, we should take the gospel to an unbelieving world with even greater urgency. If we keep our eyes firmly fixed upon Jesus we can be confident that he will bring us through whatever the future holds.

Conclusion

I think we can continue to be optimistic about the spread of the gospel. I concluded my introductory chapter by describing the tension between an optimistic outlook and a pessimistic one. If the theme of this book, the premillennial view, is correct then the outlook for the world is indeed a pessimistic one. The world at large and even many Christians are not aware of this, but that is the reality.

Those Christians who know and believe this should not be downcast. The world is still open to the spread of the gospel and many Christians report that large numbers of people are coming to Christ in many parts of the world. This is true of China and is even said to be true of Iran.

We are yet to see it in Europe. I reproduce here an amazing prophecy that is thought to have been given by the famous evangelist Smith Wigglesworth a few months before his death in 1947.[5] God had given Smith Wigglesworth a powerful evangelistic and healing ministry. Here was a man who really had seen revival and the miraculous work of the Holy Spirit, both in Britain and in other countries. This is what he said:

> *During the next few decades there will be two distinct moves of the Holy Spirit across the Church in Great Britain. The first move will affect every church that is open to receive it and will be characterised by restoration of the baptism and gifts of the Holy Spirit.*
>
> *The second move of the Holy Spirit will result in people leaving historic churches and planting new churches.*
>
> *In the duration of each of these moves, the people who are involved will say 'This is a great revival.' But the Lord says 'No, neither is this the great revival but both are steps towards it.' When the new church phase is on the wane, there will be evidenced in the churches something that has not been seen before: a coming together of those with an emphasis on the Word and those with an emphasis on the Spirit.*
>
> *When the Word and the Spirit come together, there will be the biggest movement of the Holy Spirit that the nation, and indeed, the world has ever seen. It will mark the beginning of a revival that will eclipse anything that has been witnessed within these shores, even the Wesleyan and the Welsh revivals of former years. The outpouring of God's Spirit will flow over from the United Kingdom to the mainland of Europe, and from there, will begin a missionary move to the ends of the earth.*

This prophecy sounds authentic and is certainly optimistic. The first part of the prophecy has come to pass. I came to faith in the first of the two moves. I have experienced the charismatic revival and I have witnessed the planting of new churches in the United Kingdom.

The final part of the prophecy has not yet happened. It speaks of God favouring Britain once again as he did in the nineteenth century, with taking the gospel to mainland Europe. From Britain and Europe it will then spread like a ripple across the world.

There are signs that churches across the United Kingdom are beginning to plant churches in Europe[6]. This is still in its infancy, but I was intrigued and delighted to learn that my own church, quite independently of others, has recently felt led to plant churches in two large European cities. This revival, if the Wigglesworth prophecy is from God, could eclipse the evil in the world. It could be a final burst of God's glorious light before the coming darkness. Alternatively it could happen in parallel to the growing darkness. Either way, God's plan to save many more souls is good news indeed.

NOTES

1. The USA, USSR, Britain, France and China were recognised as nuclear states at the start of the treaty. Since that time India, Pakistan and North Korea have openly declared the possession of nuclear weapons. They either never signed the treaty or have withdrawn from it. Israel has never acknowledged possession of such weapons, but is recognised by all to possess them. Its secrecy may be part of its declared policy never to be the first to use weapons of mass destruction (chemical, biological or nuclear) in a conflict. Despite its denial Iran is now thought to be very close to developing nuclear weapons and the means to deliver them. Once it declares possession of nuclear weapons or the ability to produce them this will destabilise the Middle East. Nations such as Saudi Arabia will feel obliged to follow suit.

2. Both Ayatollah Ali Khamenei, the spiritual leader of Iran and the former President Mahmoud Ahmadinejad have indicated their wish to see Israel removed as a nation and the land revert to a Muslim state. A search of the Internet reveals the Iranian leaders' open hostility towards Israel, although some commentators argue about exactly what has been said. One of the most objective statements was that given by the former Spanish Prime Minister José Aznar in a speech quoted by the *Jerusalem Post*, 16 July 2012:

<http://www.jpost.com/Diplomacy-and-Politics/Putin-said-Israel-would-take-care-of-Iran >

3. God is not responsible for their use. Mankind will be responsible, with incitement from Satan. I recognise, of course, that atomic bombs were used against Japan at the end of World War II, but their very destructiveness has to date been one of the factors restraining the further use of such weapons.

4. This possibility was discussed in an article, 'PA will dismantle itself and Hamas can fill the gap' by Nathan Jeffay (*Jewish Chronicle*, 11 April 2014). One of the leading proponents is Tareq Abbas, son of the Palestinian President Mahmoud Abbas.

5. A search of the Internet will reveal, as with so many spiritual matters, that there is disagreement about the origin of this prophecy. However, Wigglesworth is known to have given a similar prophecy to David du Plessis in South Africa in 1936, while other leaders such as Jean Darnall and Derek Prince have also given prophecies along these lines. The most important thing is that the first part of the prophecy has been fulfilled after the event and therefore satisfies God's requirement concerning the authenticity of a prophecy (see *Deuteronomy 18:21-22*). We should have every confidence that the rest of it will be fulfilled.

6. A search of the Internet will reveal inter-church organisations such as *Acts 29 Europe* which are beginning to plant churches in European cities. Likewise there are evangelists such as David Hathaway, whose work has led to the planting of churches in Eastern Europe and Russia.

POSTSCRIPT

Dear Reader,

It is possible that you are not a Christian and that you have read this book out of interest or because a Christian friend has lent it to you. If that is the case, can I ask you to consider the message of Salvation through Jesus Christ? Although evangelical Christians may disagree on the end-times, they are united about the need to have faith in the risen Jesus Christ, the same Jesus who, as this book explains, will one day return to the earth.

Whatever happens in the coming years, we can have no greater security than that obtained by putting our faith in Christ. Whether our future on earth will be difficult or not, we have the certainty of spending eternity with Christ when we believe and put our trust in him.

I would urge you to think about the following prayer and if you can pray it sincerely, then please pray it confidently, preferably out loud! This is all you have to do to be reconciled to God and to become a born-again Christian.

Once you have prayed the prayer then I urge you to make contact with a Christian or a church and tell them of your decision. You will have made the decision that determines your eternal destiny, but you will need to grow as a Christian through reading the Bible and having fellowship with other Christians.

I wish you well in your Christian life.

Mark Dunman
(website: *markdunman.com*)

The prayer of salvation

Heavenly Father, I now understand that I have sinned against you. I understand too that you sent Jesus to die on the Cross for my sins and that you raised him from the dead. I am truly sorry for my sins. I repent of them and ask you to forgive me.

I now ask Jesus to come into my life and renew my spirit so that I may have eternal life. I ask Jesus to take charge of my life as my Saviour and Lord. Thank you for my salvation.

APPENDIX 1
THE BIBLE'S MEASUREMENT OF TIME

For the most part this is straightforward – a day means a day and a year means a year. There are, however, two aspects of biblical time that need explanation. These are the number of days in a year and the prophet Daniel's 70 weeks (*Daniel 9:24-27*).

Number of days in a year

Ancient civilisations and the Hebrew Bible worked according to a 360-day year. This is confirmed very clearly in Genesis at the time of the Noahic Flood (see *Genesis 7:11* to *8:5*). The flood waters started on the 17th day of the second month and the ark came to rest on the mountains of Ararat on the 17th day of the seventh month, also described as 150 days. From this we can see that 5 months = 150 days and so 1 month = 30 days. A search of the Internet will reveal several possible explanations as to why the ancient calendar was different from the present solar calendar of 365.25 days. Whatever happened at the time of the Flood seems to have caused the earth to spin more rapidly so that on its annual journey around the sun it completed more daily revolutions, each day being slightly shorter than before this change.[1]

After the Flood it seems that ancient civilisations continued to use the 360-day year even though their astronomers were able to work out the actual days in a year, and then adjust it by inserting intercalary days at the end of the year or at the end of certain months.

We can now see how the time interval: *time, times and half a time* in *Daniel 7:25* matches the time interval in Revelation. The expressions *time, times and half a time*, *42 months* and *1260 days* all mean the same and are equal to three and a half 360-day years (*Revelation 12:6, 14; 13:5*). The repetition of this time interval in both books makes a striking connection between them.

Daniel's seventy weeks

Daniel's 70 weeks (*Daniel 9:24-27*) is a very accurate prophecy, but it must be understood that the 'weeks' are weeks of seven years. It has been calculated that it predicts the time of Christ's crucifixion very accurately. The seventy weeks are to start from the order to restore and build Jerusalem. This order was given by King Artaxerxes of Medo-Persia to Nehemiah in 444 or 445 BC. *'An anointed one'* is said to be cut off (*verse 26*) after 69 (7 + 62) weeks. This represents 483 Hebrew years which is equivalent to 476 solar years which takes us to AD 32 or 33, the likely date of Christ's crucifixion. This is a quick resumé of a topic that has been studied in much more detail by various authors.[2]

It is important that we should understand and be confident about the meaning of Daniel's 70 weeks because for premillennialists it is the seventieth week from which we get the Tribulation interval of seven years. The fact that there must be a long hiatus (the Church age) between the 69th and 70th week causes difficulties for many theologians and Bible students. What they fail to realise, however, is that Daniel's prophecy is about his people, the Jews, not about the Church, and only incidentally about the Gentiles. When we tie this in with Jesus' Olivet discourse and the book of Revelation, it makes perfect sense that this 70th week is yet in the future.

Thus the significance of the 360-day year and the meaning of Daniel's 'week' becomes apparent.

One day and a thousand years

There is one more topic that is worth mentioning. Some authors see significance in the connection made between one day and a thousand years. The apostle Peter appears to be quoting *Psalm 90:4* when he says:

> ... *with the Lord one day is as a thousand years, and a thousand years as one day.*
>
> *(2 Peter 3:8)*

This may simply be a statement about God's thought processes, or it may have a deeper relevance to God's calendar. Some writers make the connection between a week of seven days with the seventh day being a day of rest, and a period of 7000 years with the last 1000 years, also representing a time of rest. This would make the history of the earth (or recreated earth)[3] 7000 years (6000 years to date) with the last 1000 corresponding to the Millennium.

This is an intriguing idea, because I do believe that time and schedules are much more important to God than we generally realise. However, I have not pursued the idea, because I do not think the evidence is strong enough to establish such a view. (*It should be noted that this is not the same as the dispensational view of biblical history which argues that the dispensations (often seven, but not always) are about God's plans for human government at different stages in human history and which do not necessarily match up with intervals of 1000 years.*)

NOTES

1. There is much material (and speculation) as to what might have happened
    to the earth at the time of Noah's Flood. One interesting source is Dr E.K.
    Victor Pearce and his book *Evidence for Truth: Science*, Pages 223 and 243.
    He puts forward interesting ideas on a possible shift in the earth's polar axis
    relative to the sun at the time of the Flood (from 0° to its present 23.5°) and
    how this could have caused the flood waters to rush across the earth's land
    mass. As a scientist he presents evidence, but whether this is conclusive is
    another matter.

2. Readers will find articles on the Internet which demonstrate the mathematics
    of Daniel's 70 week prophecy.

    It is only fair to add that some authors put a different interpretation on the
    unfolding of the years.

3. Another debate among Christians centres on the age of the earth, between
    those who believe the earth is around 6000 years old (young earth) and
    those who subscribe to the general scientific view that the earth is very old
    (old earth). The earth we know today would then be an old earth in which
    the 'days' of Genesis represented periods of indeterminate length or an old
    earth which had undergone a previous deluge and was recreated in seven
    days. Supporters of this latter view argue that the Bible is a book about
    the Adamic race and not about anything which may have gone before. This
    however is not the book to enter into this debate.

APPENDIX 2
THE PERMANENCE OF THE ABRAHAMIC COVENANT

The Abrahamic Covenant was a covenant given to the Jews through the patriarch Abraham for all time. We can see this clearly in the Old Testament. It was virtually an unconditional covenant on the part of God. God undertook to make an everlasting covenant with Abraham's descendants through Isaac and Jacob and to give them the land of Canaan as an everlasting possession. The only requirement on Abraham's side was the ordinance of circumcision for Abraham and his descendants. The permanence of the covenant is made irrevocably clear from two passages of Scripture.

The first is from *Jeremiah Chapter 31* and the second is from King David's Song of Thanks in *I Chronicles*:

> *Thus says the Lord, who gives the sun for light by day and the fixed order of the moon and the stars for light by night, who stirs up the sea so that its waves roar – the Lord of hosts is his name: "If this fixed order departs from before me, declares the Lord, then shall the offspring of Israel cease from being a nation before me for ever." Thus says the Lord: "If the heavens above can be measured, and the foundations of the earth below can be explored, then I will cast off all the offspring of Israel for all that they have done, declares the Lord."*
>
> (Jeremiah 31:35-37)

Remember his covenant for ever, the word that he commanded,
for a thousand generations, the covenant that he made with
Abraham, his sworn promise to Isaac, which he confirmed as
a statute to Jacob, as an everlasting covenant to Israel, saying,
"To you I will give the land of Canaan, as your portion for
an inheritance."

(I Chronicles 16:15-16)

There is no way that God would overturn the promises of these two passages of Scripture.

The confusion over the permanence of the Abrahamic Covenant arises from two sources: the consequences of the Mosaic Covenant and certain passages in the New Testament. Let us look first at the Mosaic Covenant. The argument is that the Jews forfeited their right to live in the land of Israel by breaking the Mosaic Covenant. That this would happen is stated clearly in the chapters on blessings and curses found in *Leviticus Chapter 26* and *Deuteronomy Chapters 27* and *28*. Eviction did indeed happen at the time of the two exiles, first to Babylon and then later to Rome. From this we can see that occupation of the land is conditional on obedience to God's laws, but possession of the land is unconditional in accordance with the promises made originally to Abraham. God will restore the Jews to the land at a time of his choosing sometime in the future[1]. This is why it is so important to take seriously God's promises all through the Old Testament about a restoration of the Jews.

It is sometimes said that the Abrahamic Covenant has been abrogated in the New Testament especially in the book of Hebrews when it is said that the New Covenant has superseded or made obsolete the Old Covenant, for example in *Hebrews Chapters 7, 8* and *9*. The Old or Mosaic Covenant has indeed been superseded by the New Covenant, but in *Chapter 6* where the author is writing about the Abrahamic Covenant, it is abundantly clear that this covenant (in contrast to the Mosaic Covenant) is still very much in place (see *Hebrews 6:13-18*). The Old Covenant is not an umbrella term for both the Abrahamic and the Mosaic Covenants; it is only applicable to the Mosaic Covenant.

The other argument is based on New Testament scriptures and in particular *Romans Chapter 4* and *Galatians Chapter 3*. Certain verses are used to argue that all believers in Jesus, Gentile and Jew, are heirs to Christ through Abraham. God's promises to Abraham are no longer restricted to Jews and so the promise of the land is no longer restricted to Israel. The land is now considered to have become the whole earth, the domain of believers, whether Jewish or Gentile. What advocates of this view miss is that this does not rescind God's original promises to Abraham concerning the Jewish people, but rather extends them to people who come to faith in God, whether Jewish or Gentile. God valued Abraham as a man of faith and it is this quality as applied to all believers that is being honoured in these passages. The Abrahamic Covenant had the dual aspect of benefitting his descendants through the flesh and his 'children' through faith in the Lord Jesus Christ.

One writer[2] has described the New Testament's extension of Abraham's faith to all believers as the international aspect of the Abrahamic Covenant. The national or ethnic aspect of the covenant is still in place for the Jewish people, though like Gentiles they must come to a belief in Christ in order to receive the benefits of the New Covenant.

NOTES

1. This restoration of the Jews to their ancient land is what many Christians believe has been happening in the twentieth century and is continuing to happen today.

2. David Pawson makes this point very clearly in his book *Defending Christian Zionism* P.61-62.

APPENDIX 3
INTERPRETATION: RULE OF DOUBLE REFERENCE

This is a very important rule of biblical interpretation. It says that a passage of scripture may be speaking of two persons or events which are separated by a long interval of time, but written as though they are fused into one picture.

The only way to assess this is to analyse the passage for distinct, irreconcilable differences. If such differences exist then we can presume that the passage refers to more than one person or event. The three passages where this is most important for understanding the end-times are *Matthew Chapter 24* (the Olivet discourse), *Daniel Chapter 9* and *Daniel Chapter 11*.

Preterists tend to presume that the Olivet discourse, Daniel's prophecies and the book of Revelation refer to events that happened at the time of the destruction of the Second Temple in AD 70. To do this they have to ignore many verses which do not fit this thesis.

Daniel Chapter 9 (verses 24-27)
Let us start with this passage. We have already seen that Daniel is talking about his people, the Jews (*Daniel 9:24*) when the angel Gabriel tells him that 70 weeks are decreed concerning his people. The first 69 weeks are consecutive as we saw in Appendix 1, but the 70th week is not. Many Christian writers have difficulty placing a gap or parenthesis between weeks 69 and 70. They cannot contemplate the Church age as filling the gap. We need to remember however that this prophecy is about the Jews. It is not about the Church. There is absolutely no

reason implicit in *Daniel 9:24-27* which says there cannot be gap of indeterminate length between the 69th and 70th week.

Furthermore, if we say that the 70th week occurs at the time of the destruction of the Temple in AD 70, there is still a parenthesis between the Crucifixion, the end of the 69th week, (circa AD 33) and the destruction of the Temple. A consecutive seven years would take us to AD 40 which is not recorded as a year of significance for the Jews.

The double reference comes between *verses 26* and *27*. It concerns the time of the two events. A superficial reading suggests that, *"the Prince who is to come"* makes a covenant with the people for the 70th week (*"for one week"*) immediately after the destruction of the city and the sanctuary, but this is not what it says. The destruction in question can certainly refer to AD 70, but it should be noted that this destruction is caused by the people of the prince who is to come, **not by the prince himself**. These people were the Romans, but we cannot presume that their leader, the Roman General Titus, was this prince. This prince, whom many consider to be the Antichrist, has not yet made *"a covenant with many"* for the remaining week of seven years. This is still in the future. Why can he not be the Roman General Titus? The answer is that Titus did not make a covenant with the Jews or anyone else, he did not set himself up as God in the Temple (see later); instead he ruthlessly ransacked and destroyed the Temple and drove the Jews into exile. This does not fit this prince of *verses 24-27*.

However, because this prince (Antichrist) who has not yet come, is said to come from the people who would destroy the Temple and the city, many Christians believe that the Antichrist will arise from a country within the Old Roman Empire. This was an extensive empire and so he could arise from one of many places – he does not have to come from Rome itself.

There is one further point to make about this passage. The time of the prophecy follows the crucifixion of Jesus (*the anointed one shall be cut off*). This means that the prince to come cannot be identified with Antiochus Epiphanes who lived well before the time of Christ. He desecrated the Temple in 167 BC and died three years later.

This example shows clearly how we can analyse the verses associated with a double reference to demonstrate what they cannot mean, and thus to narrow down what they are likely to mean.

Daniel Chapter 11 (verses 21-45) and also Chapter 12

The second example of the rule of double reference is found in *Daniel 11:21-45*. The dividing point for the double reference is *verse 35*. This is a transition verse because it introduces the phrase *"until the time of the end"* which *"still awaits the appointed time"*.

Verses 21-34 go into great prophetic detail about a king (a contemptible person) who can clearly be identified as Antiochus Epiphanes. This identification is explored fully by F.J. Dake in his Annotated Bible[1] and much of his information is derived from the historical book of *I Maccabees*, found in the Old Testament Apocrypha. Antiochus Epiphanes is a type or forerunner of the prince or king who is yet to come. He desecrates the Temple by sacrificing a pig on the altar. This is the **first** *"abomination that makes desolate"* (*Daniel 11:31*).

However, *verse 36* moves on to describe a king who is very different from Antiochus Epiphanes. He exalts and magnifies himself above every god. After a description of his character and activities we learn (in *Chapter 12*) that the angel Michael, who keeps watch over Israel, will arise at a time of trouble, the like of which has not been seen before. At this time, the time of the end, a **second** *"abomination that makes desolate"* will take place (*Daniel 12:11*). We know for certain that this is not the same as the abomination of Antiochus, because Jesus refers to this abomination as being in the future (*Matthew 24:15*) whereas the abomination of Antiochus is now in the past, having happened in 167 BC.

It is by this kind of analysis that we can rightly divide the double reference of this second passage.

Matthew Chapter 24 (The Olivet discourse)

Let us now turn to *Matthew Chapter 24*. Jesus' discourse to his disciples on the Mount of Olives was clearly related many centuries after the time of Daniel and after many, but not all of Daniel's prophecies had been fulfilled.

It is said by preterists that most if not all of both Daniel's and Jesus' prophecies were fulfilled in the destruction of the Temple and Jerusalem in the time around AD 70. However, we have seen that Daniel talks about the time of the end and about a trouble greater than the world had ever seen. Bad as the period AD 66-70 was, it did not fulfil the time of the end or the apocalyptic nature of this time.

Jesus begins *Matthew Chapter 24* by a clear reference to the destruction of the Temple which did indeed happen in AD 70 following the Jewish revolt. However, the disciples then go on to ask him about the close of the age and the return of himself, two events that did not happen in AD 70 and still have not happened 2000 years later. The dividing line in the double reference on this occasion comes between *verses 1* and *2* and the rest of the chapter.

From *verses 3* to *31* Jesus is talking about the close of the age, not about the destruction of the Temple in AD 70. It is possible that the flight of Jewish Christians to Pella in Jordan at the time of the destruction of the Temple was prompted by Jesus' words in *verses 16-21*, but Jesus was talking about a flight in the end-times. The destruction of the Temple by Titus was not the abomination of desolation spoken of either by Daniel or Jesus. Titus destroyed rather than desecrated the Temple and he did not set himself up as God. Jesus goes on to describe a tribulation far more extensive than the destruction of Jerusalem (*verse 21*), one which apart from the intervention of God, no human life would survive.

The apostle Paul talks about the man of lawlessness taking his seat in the Temple of God and proclaiming himself to be God. This is the abomination of desolation spoken of by Daniel (*Daniel 12:11*) and by Jesus in *Matthew 24:15*. It could be that the image of the beast (*Revelation 13:14-15*) itself is set up in the Temple. It is not unreasonable to argue that this abomination refers to the Antichrist, the prince who is yet to come.

Thus although *Matthew Chapter 24* starts with the destruction of the Temple, it quickly moves on to the close of the age. It is incomplete exegesis to run *verses 1-2* into the rest of the chapter as though they refer to the same thing, just as it is incomplete exegesis to consider *Daniel Chapter 11* as referring to only one king.

I hope the reader can now see that the biblical rule of double reference is not a convenient, made-up belief, but one which is real and is necessary to understand some of the biblical prophecies relating to the end-times.

NOTES

1. *Dake's Annotated Reference Bible*, F.J. Dake P.870 Notes to Daniel Chapter 11, column 4.

APPENDIX 4
TABLE OF MOTHER AND SON DEITIES

The theme of *mother and son*, goddess and god clearly runs through many pagan religions and has sadly found its modern counterpart as the Madonna and Child of the Roman Catholic Church. I have however, limited this list to a few of the better-known examples.

There is a multiplicity of gods and goddesses in pagan religions, and their relationships and their names change as the legend changes. Authors do not always distinguish fact from fiction.

I am convinced that pagan worship began in Babylon with Nimrod and that the legend of Nimrod, Semiramis and Tammuz (although not established factually) is as a good a starting point as any other. However, once we get to the Greek and Roman gods and goddesses, there are simply too many to identify a link between the original *mother and son* to those in the Greek and Roman Pantheon. Semiramis is said to have become transformed into numerous female Greek goddesses, responsible for fertility, motherhood and nature.

I mention the Phoenician gods in the table for two reasons:

1. Geographically Phoenicia covered the northern part of Canaan (modern-day Lebanon and the north of Israel) and its religion of Babylonian origin impacted the Israelites. It provided the essentials of the Canaanite religion.

2. Phoenicia was a great seafaring nation and thus the claim that it transferred the elements of its religion to other nations around the Mediterranean has a basis in fact.

It is important to remember that in some of these pagan religions the *father and son* are interchangeable. The son often imitates Jesus, the true Son of God, in some aspect: he may be born of a virgin, be resurrected or be a saviour to the world. Statuettes often show the goddess with a male child.

Greek and Roman gods have been excluded, both because of their multiplicity and because the relationship between gods and humans is mixed up. For example, the relationship between the Greek: Aphrodite and Dionysius (Eros) or the equivalent Roman: Venus and Adonis (Cupid) seem simply to be an erotic human tale given mythical status. That is certainly how the Renaissance painters perceived it!

Religion	Goddess* (Mother)	God* (as Son)	Paternal God*	Biblical and Other Sources
Babylon	Semiramis (Queen of Heaven, Ishtar)	Tammuz (Ninus)	Nimrod (Bel, Marduk, Merodoch)	*Isaiah 46:1 Jeremiah 50:2 (Hebrew)*
Egypt	Isis	Horus	Osiris	
Canaan (including Phoenicia)	Ashtoreth (Astarte)	Tammuz (Baal)	Baal (El, Molech)	Frequent biblical References
India	Isi (Devaki)	Iswara (Krishna)	Vishnu	
China	Shing-moo	Yi	Pan-Ku	
Mexico (Aztecs)	Coatlicue	Quetzalcoatl	Ometeotl	
Scandinavia and Germany	Frigga (Fregga)	Balder	Odin	Overlapping between the Norse and Teutonic gods
	Nerthus (Hertha)	Frey	Njord	
Europe	Europa (Greek goddess)		Sacred bull (symbol of Baal)	Europa has been adopted as a symbol of the European Union
Druids (Northern Europe)	Virgo-Partitura	(meaning a virgin about to give birth)		

* Alternative names or similar gods, given in parentheses.

APPENDIX 5
THE EZEKIEL TEMPLE

Some readers will know that the Temple described by Ezekiel (*Chapters 40-46*) presents a dilemma for many Christians. It describes the reinstitution of animal sacrifices in a Temple that is to be built in the Millennium following the return of Jesus Christ. The dilemma is understandable because the New Testament makes it abundantly clear that Christ came on his first visit to earth to be the ultimate sacrifice for human sin and to abolish the animal sacrifices of the Mosaic Covenant. This had only ever been a temporary covering for sin, never a solution. Animal sacrifices never did away with sin; only the blood of the sinless Son of God could do that.

Is there an explanation for this reinstitution of animal sacrifices after the return of Christ, while he is present in Jerusalem during the Millennium?

Sacrifices as a memorial to the Mosaic Covenant

Premillennial writers tend to answer this question by describing the sacrifices as a memorial of what used to happen before Christ's once and for all sacrifice on the Cross. This view is neatly summed up in the following quotation:

*Most premillennial scholars agree that the purpose of animal
sacrifice during the millennial kingdom is memorial in nature.
As the Lord's Supper is a reminder of the death of Christ to
the Church today, animal sacrifices will be a reminder during
the millennial kingdom. To those born during the millennial
kingdom, animal sacrifices will again be an object lesson. During
that future time, righteousness and holiness will prevail, but
those with earthly bodies will still have a sin nature and there
will be a need to teach about how offensive sin is to a holy and
righteous God. Animal sacrifices will serve that purpose, "but
in those sacrifices there is a reminder of sins year by year"
(Hebrews 10:3)[1]*

Many Christians are not satisfied with this explanation, not least
because Ezekiel describes the sacrifices as sin offerings to make
atonement on behalf of the house of Israel (*Ezekiel Chapters 45:16-17*).
These sacrifices are also referred to briefly at the end of Zechariah
(*Zechariah 14:20-21*), a passage which clearly follows the return of the
Lord to Jerusalem.

Ezekiel's Temple failed to be constructed

The alternative approach is to argue that Ezekiel's Temple is not
a description of a temple to be built in a future millennium, but a
blueprint for a temple that did not get built. It was meant to be a
blueprint for the Second Temple built by Zerubbabel or at least for
the refurbished temple built by Herod the Great, which he started in
19 BC.

There is an ingenious article by T.H. Whitehouse[2] which suggests
that the order of the chapters in Ezekiel does not follow the
historical sequence in which they were written. He states that the
chapters about Israel's restoration and the rebuilding of the Temple
(*Ezekiel 31-48*) were written before the chapters which are much
more critical of Israel (*Ezekiel Chapters 31-48*). His hypothesis is that
Israel was given a divine scheme for renewal: in territory, government
and temple worship which through their continuing sinfulness they

failed to achieve. God withheld the fulfilment of this plan. Here is a quotation from Whitehouse's article:

> *Therefore, in fact, the last nine chapters of the book are not millennial, and so do not contradict the Gospel of Yeshua the Messiah! They are the record of a Divine scheme of renewal – tentatively offered for the free choice or rejection of Israel – but made wholly dependent on the subjection of their will and the change of their heart towards Yehovah God – which, however, was unhappily not realised. Therefore, since the imperative conditions were not met, the offer lapsed, the scheme became inoperative, and Israel's dispersion inevitably had to be inflicted.*
>
> *But so interesting and important a document could not be allowed to be lost or destroyed. It had to be preserved as a witness to Yehovah's righteous and pitiful dealings with His unworthy people. Accordingly it was duly dated and retained among the other documents left by Ezekiel, and when they were afterwards put into volume form it was relegated to a place at the end of the Book as an appendix. But – since it bears no outward description as an appendix, and was placed in a position immediately following upon chapters which foretell the final tribulation period and the ending at the "Presence" of the Lord – it has unfortunately been commonly but wrongly assumed to foretell a continuation of the historical developments of those chapters and to be therefore Millennial – which it most certainly is not!*

However ingenious this idea may be, it does not stand up to scrutiny for several reasons, some of which I give here:

1. *Zechariah Chapter 14* describes the return of the Lord Jesus to vanquish his foes and how after this, the nations will go up to worship him in Jerusalem year after year. This worship will include sacrifices (*Zechariah 14:20-21*).

2. Zechariah also describes in this same chapter how fresh (living) waters will flow out from Jerusalem to the Dead Sea, exactly as described in Ezekiel from under the rebuilt Temple (*Ezekiel 47:1-12*).

To believe that the Temple is provisional is to accept that the prophesied major topographical changes at the time of Christ's return are also provisional. The reality is that the chapters about a rebuilt temple are intimately tied in with the topographical changes and the redistribution of land to the tribes of Israel.

3. Although Herod is believed to have wanted to model his refurbishing and expansion of the Second Temple according to Ezekiel's plans, there are major differences in the design and functioning of the two temples.

4. The idea that the implementation of the new Temple, the tribal division of the land and major topographical change were conditional on Israel's change of heart towards God is unrealistic. God knew that Israel was sinful (just like the Gentile nations) which is why he introduced the New Covenant (*Jeremiah 31:31-34*) in which he himself would bring about the changes required, as described so clearly in *Ezekiel Chapters 36:22-33 and 37:14 & 23*.

5. The idea that chapters describing these events have been retained in Ezekiel as an important appendix, even though they were never implemented, is stretching credulity. The detail concerning the rebuilding and practice of the Temple is as great as that for the Tabernacle (*Exodus Chapters 25 to 30*) and more than that for Solomon's Temple (*1 Kings Chapters 5 and 6*). Both the Tabernacle and Solomon's Temple were built and there is no reason to think that Ezekiel's Temple will not also be built.

Conclusion

What then are we to make of the sacrifices? I can add nothing by way of explanation: I do not know God's reasons. All I can say personally is that if Ezekiel's Temple is a future temple, as I am convinced it is, then I am prepared to accept the literal truth of God's Word. I will not try and change the meaning of the text through interpretation. As the apostle Paul says: *"For now we see through a glass, darkly; but then face to face: now I know in part; but then shall I know even as also I am known."* *(1 Corinthians 13:12 KJV)*. It is one of those situations where we will have to await an explanation.

A Google search will reveal several interesting websites on this topic of Ezekiel's Temple.

NOTES

1. Website: <http://www.gotquestions.org/millennial-sacrifices.html>

2. Article by T.H. Whitehouse: *Ezekiel's Temple and Sacrifices: will Temple sacrifices resume in the Millennium?* Website: <hope-of-israel.org.nz/ezekielstemple.html>

GLOSSARY

Allegory is an extended metaphor. There is a sense of an unfolding story. For example, Jesus Christ is described as the Lion of the Tribe of Judah (*Revelation 5:5*). This is a simple metaphor. On the other hand the Valley of Dry Bones in *Ezekiel Chapter 37* is an allegory for the restoration of the nation of Israel. The story unfolds as the bones come to life and we are told that they represent the whole house of Israel.

Apocalypse (lit. *unveiling*) is the prophetic revelation given to the Apostle John as recorded in the book of *Revelation*. **Apocalyptic** means pertaining to this revelation; prophesying disaster or doom.

Apostasy means falling away from the Christian faith. It can also be used in relation to other faiths and political causes.

Canon of Scripture is the list of books considered to be inspired by the Holy Spirit and which therefore constitute the Bible as we know it today. The process of consolidating the canon was spread over time. The Old Testament canon (which the Jews call the *Tanakh*) was thought to have been completed by the end of the first century AD, possibly at a Council of Jamnia circa AD 90. The New Testament canon (of 27 books), however, was not settled until the end of the fourth century AD, where it was accepted as closed at the Council of Carthage in AD 397 under the leadership of St. Augustine.

Charismatic Revival refers to the Holy Spirit Renewal in the traditional churches from the middle of the twentieth century. This led to Christians being 'baptised in the Holy Spirit' with the accompaniment of supernatural gifts such as prophecy and 'speaking in tongues'. It had been preceded by the Pentecostal awakening earlier in the century with the establishment of Pentecostal denominations.

Church Fathers were the leading Christian theologians in the early centuries of the Church, ending with St. Augustine in the fourth century AD. They were especially significant in Church history as they formulated doctrine in the years before the *Canon of Scripture* was finalised.

Dispensationalism is the theology which divides biblical history into distinct periods or ages, (most commonly seven). Each dispensation represents a different way in which God works with mankind in salvation history. The last two: 'the Church age' and 'the Kingdom (Millennial) age' are the two relevant ages to a contemporary view of Israel. Dispensationalists tend to think the Church age has run its course and that God has now turned his attention back to Israel. (Some writers – this author included – would argue that the theology of the Church and Israel does not have to be an 'either the Church or Israel' theology. It can be both.)

Eschatology is the doctrine of the end-times, both preceding and following Christ's return to earth.

Evangelical Christian is one who has had a personal encounter with the risen Jesus Christ and who feels motivated to share the Good News.

Exegesis is the explanation or interpretation of Scripture.

Great Tribulation (Jacob's Trouble): This term is sometimes used to describe the second half of the Tribulation. It comes from Jesus' description of this period as a terrible time of trouble (*Matthew 24:21*) in which the Antichrist turns against the Jews.

Hermeneutics denotes the art and science of text interpretation. In biblical hermeneutics, the *allegorical, typological* and *literal* would be different ways of understanding Scripture.

Literalism: This refers to the *hermeneutic* whereby prophetic scripture is understood to have a literal, rather than an allegorical meaning.

Messianic Jew: These are Jews who have come to a personal faith in Jesus Christ as their saviour and messiah. They are in God's family along with Gentile Christians, but prefer to be known as Messianic believers as a means of retaining their identity as Jews.

Metaphor is a figure of speech in which one object (or being) is described as another object (or being) in order to illustrate or emphasise its nature. For example, Jesus describes himself as the vine and believers as its branches.

Millennium: See Chapter 2.

Mosaic Law: This was the set of laws and commands given by God to the Israelites through Moses for governing every aspect of their lives. It was headed by the Moral Law or Ten Commandments and consisted in total of 613 statutes (mitzvot) including the two Genesis commands, "be fruitful and multiply" and male circumcision.

New Covenant: The New Covenant was first announced for the Jews in *Jeremiah 31:31-34*. It was enacted when Jesus died on the Cross for the sins of mankind and was subsequently resurrected. For those who accept this sacrifice on their behalf, both Jew and Gentile, God gives them a new heart and writes his law upon it. It both fulfils and takes the place of the Old (Mosaic) Covenant.

New Heavens and Earth: This concerns the promise of God that the existing heavens and earth will be burnt up and new ones created in their place. It is referred to in both the Old Testament (*Isaiah 65:17* and *66:22*) and the New Testament (*2 Peter 3:7* and *Revelation 21:1*).

Old Covenant: This is the covenant inaugurated between God and Moses who represented the Israelites. It is often called the *Mosaic Law* and is not to be confused with the Abrahamic Covenant. It set down the rules by which the Israelites should govern their relationship with God and between themselves, as the people were about to enter statehood as a nation.

Olivet Discourse: This was Jesus' talk to his disciples about the last days, prior to his crucifixion (See *Matthew Chapter 24* and *25; Luke Chapter 21*).

Paganism: The word pagan relates to religion derived from nature and the material world. Paganism rejects monotheistic religion. It tends to believe in a plurality of gods (polytheism) and to ascribe a living soul to inanimate objects (animism). It ranges from celebrating nature to full involvement in the occult. **Pagan practices** in the Old Testament were often morally repugnant, and abhorrent to God.

Parable is an allegorical narrative of real or imagined events from which a moral is drawn for the listener. The Parable was a popular teaching method with Jesus.

Pentecost (Feast of Weeks, Hebrew *Shavuot*): The Day of Pentecost was the occasion described in *Acts Chapter 2* when the Holy Spirit fell on the assembled disciples of Jesus and they were supernaturally empowered to 'speak in tongues' and to preach the gospel. In modern times **Pentecostal** has come to mean the reappearance of the experience of the Baptism in the Holy Spirit in the Christian Church, such as happened in the *Acts of the Apostles*. Churches espousing this experience are called Pentecostal.

Preterism: See Chapter 2, note 5.

Progressive Parallelism is the symbolic scheme which sees the book of Revelation as consisting of seven sections running parallel to each other. All seven sections are said to reveal some aspect of the Church's relationship to Christ, the world and the devil. Although parallel, the seven sections are said to exhibit some eschatological progress, the last section clearly referring to the triumph of Christ over his enemies; hence the name *progressive* parallelism.

Prophecy in the Bible is a supernatural revelation from God. It may reveal his heart for his people or his views on a subject, or it may be a message revealing future events. In the time of the Old Testament, speaking through **Prophets** was God's way of warning Israel, and urging them to return to him and his laws.

Protestant Church: This was the Church which emerged from the break with the Catholic Church during the Reformation in the sixteenth century. The Reformation, spearheaded by Martin Luther, affirmed the principles of **justification by faith alone** (i.e. not by good works), **the priesthood of all believers** and **the authority of the Bible** as God's revealed word to humanity. The Reformation encouraged people to read the Bible for themselves. It did away with the mediatory role of the priests and the idolatry of Mary, the mother of Jesus. It encouraged believers to relate directly to God in prayer, within the context of Church authority. There are today many denominations within the Protestant Church who vary in aspects of theology or Church practice, but all subscribe to this overarching theology.

Replacement Theology holds that the promises concerning Israel in the Old Testament find their fulfilment in Christ and/or the Church in the New Testament. It is an alternative term for *Supersessionism* and *Fulfilment Theology*.

Salvation is the process whereby we recognise that we are sinners in the sight of a holy God, and accept his solution through the death of Jesus Christ on the Cross. When we do this we are forgiven our sin, and our spirit is regenerated by the Holy Spirit. We are saved from judgement by God and said to be 'born-again' to spend eternity with him.

Seleucid Kings: Following the death of Alexander the Great at a young age in 323 BC, the vast Greek Empire was left without an heir. After years of strife among his generals it became divided into several sub-kingdoms. The two kingdoms pertinent to the Holy Land were the Ptolemaic dynasty in Egypt to the south (under Ptolemy I) and the Seleucid dynasty over Syria and Asia Minor to the north (under Seleucus I). A succession of Ptolemaic and Seleucid kings vied for and exercised influence over the Holy Land during this time. One of the most infamous Seleucid kings was Antiochus IV Epiphanes who desecrated the Jewish Temple and tried to eradicate Judaism. This led to the revolt of the Maccabees in 167 BC and to an independent or semi-independent Jewish state for 100 years. The once extensive Seleucid empire was defeated by the Persians from the East, while the Roman General Pompey defeated them from the West turning Syria into a province of the Roman Empire.

Sorcery is witchcraft or deep participation in the occult.

Supersessionism: See *Replacement Theology.*

Tabernacle: The Tabernacle was the tent of meeting between God and his people. Moses was given instructions about how to build this on Mount Sinai, while the Israelites were still en route to the Promised Land. The system of Priests and Levites (assistant priests) together with the extensive system of animal sacrifice were all instituted for the Tabernacle. The presence of God dwelt in the inner sanctum, the Holy of Holies. The Tabernacle was later replaced by a permanent building, the *Temple.*

Temple: The Temple was central to Jewish belief and practice in the Old Testament. It took the place of the Tabernacle, first built while the Israelites were still on the move. King David desired to build a permanent home as a dwelling place for the Lord's presence, but this privilege was granted to his son, Solomon, who built the magnificent **First Temple**. This embodied the system of Priests and Levites and all the practices which belonged to the Tabernacle. This Temple was destroyed by Nebuchadnezzar when the people of Judah went into exile in Babylon. It was rebuilt as the **Second Temple** under the leadership of Zerubbabel when the Jews were allowed to return after seventy years of exile. (This Temple was completed circa 516 BC.) Although built to replicate the First Temple, it lacked certain items such as the Ark of the Covenant and the Tablets of Stone which had been lost at the time of the First Temple's destruction. According to Jewish tradition, it also lacked the Shekinah glory or Presence of God. This Temple was then enlarged and made more magnificent by Herod the Great in the first century BC. The Second Temple was the one destroyed by the Romans in AD 70.

Theocracy is government directly from God, mediated by priests. This was the government instituted by God for the Israelites through Moses. God was disappointed and offended when the Israelites sought a king to rule over them during the time of Samuel, but they were still bound by the Mosaic Law.

Theology is the in-depth study of the Jewish and Christian faiths. It deals with God's nature, his attributes and his relationship to his creation. It uses the Bible as its primary source.

Typology is a *hermeneutic* in which Old Testament 'types' are seen as being fulfilled in the New Testament. For example, Joseph is seen as a 'type' to represent Jesus, while the prospective sacrifice of Isaac by his father Abraham is seen as a 'type' for the crucifixion of God's Son. It does not exclude a *literalist* hermeneutic running parallel to a typological one.

Zion/Mount Zion: This term has several meanings:

The rocky escarpment first captured by King David from the Jebusites on which he founded the original City of David. In Jerusalem this is situated to the south of Mount Moriah, or the Temple Mount.

The City of Jerusalem itself.

Israel as a nation.

BIBLIOGRAPHY

There is a mass of literature available on the end of the age and the return of Jesus Christ including numerous articles on the Internet. Readers might find that the best way to tackle the subject is to read comparative accounts of the different approaches. Towards this end I recommend three books:

Kyle, Richard, *Awaiting the Millennium* (Leicester: IVP 1998)
This gives a good summary of the history of end-times thinking, from the start of the Church age.

Clouse, Robert G, *The Meaning of the Millennium* (Downers Grove, IL: IVP Academic 1977)
This very popular book presents articles on the four principal millennial views by four authors (Ladd, Hoyt, Boettner and Hoekema). Each of the other three authors then makes a response to each article. There is thus a very thorough examination of each millennial view.

Reiter, Richard, *Three views on the Rapture – Pre-, Mid-, or Post-Tribulation* (Grand Rapids, MI: Zondervan 1996)
This is similar to the previous book in that three authors present their view of the timing of the Rapture to which the other authors respond.

Authors mentioned in the text have written:

Boettner, Loraine, *The Millennium* (Presbyterian & Reformed 2012)

Dunman, Mark, *Has God really finished with Israel?* (London: New Wine Press 2013)

Fruchtenbaum, Arnold, *Messianic Bible Studies: The Olivet Discourse (MBS028)* and others.

(Ariel Ministries: ariel.org – under Resources, 2005)

Hendriksen, William, *More than Conquerors* (Grand Rapids, MI: Baker Books 1998)

Hoekema, Anthony, *The Bible and the Future* (Grand Rapids, MI: Eerdmans 1994)

Hoyt, Herman A, *The End Times* (John Ritchie Ltd 2000)

Kurschner, Alan, *Antichrist before the day of the Lord* (Eschatos Publishing 2013)

Ladd, G.E, *The Blessed Hope* (Grand Rapids, MI: Eerdmans 1956)

Pawson, David, *When Jesus Returns* (London: Hodder & Stoughton 2003)

There are numerous books by dispensational premillennial writers many of which give a detailed prophetic view of the unfolding events of Revelation. I have reservations about this approach, given the ease with which prophecy becomes 'established fact' among dispensationalists. However, here are three of them:

Lindsey, Hal, *The Late Great Planet Earth* (Nashville, TN: Zondervan 1970 & later)

A very popular and well-known book, but one that has had to be updated several times as prophecy has not unfolded as predicted!

Rhodes, Ron, *The End Times in Chronological Order* (Eugene, OR: Harvest House 2012)

Ellisen, Stanley. A, *Biography of a Great Planet* (Wheaton, IL: Tyndale House 1975)

As a new Christian in the 1970s I found this a clear and restrained account of the dispensational premillennial view. Used copies are still available on Amazon.

INDEX OF SCRIPTURE REFERENCES

GENERAL INDEX

204